FOOL'S JOURNEY

OR

HOW I CHASED AFTER HAPPINESS
JUST TO FIND IT WAITING FOR ME

Milena Moser

ISBN: 978-1-63491-902-9

This is a Memoir. Which means: This is what I remember. Memory is fluid, treacherous, personal. Memory is not universal truth. I am not pretending it is. In the interest of privacy, some of the names and places have been changed.

Published by BookLocker.com, Inc., St. Petersburg, Florida.

Printed on acid-free paper.

BookLocker.com, Inc.
2016

First Edition

"Das Glück sieht immer anders aus"
© Nagel & Kimche Verlag, Zürich 2015

Translated by Magdalena Zschokke
Edited by Annette PonTell
Cover Photo by Lili Tanner

For Victor who doesn't appear at all:

Love is the answer

Table of Contents

Tour Guide

I meant to go on a road trip. For years I'd been talking about it. For my 50th birthday I would take three months off and drive across the US in a rental car, completely alone, completely without a set route or goal, following only my inner voice which would say "turn right here. Stop. Stay the night." Or, "it's boring here – go on." Because my inner voice, in the course of my long and unhappily ended marriage, had gotten small and silent.

On the outside, I had it all: I was a successful writer with 18 or so books published and a weekly column that endeared me to a great many readers who followed my sometimes chaotic, but mostly charmed life. I was married and had two almost-grown sons. We lived in a dream house in a beautiful village in the middle of Switzerland after having spent 8 years in San Francisco. But inside I felt hollow. I felt like a fraud. My marriage was increasingly lonely and I felt out of place in my own home. In my homeland too. Worst of all, I couldn't even hear myself think. Hence the idea of going on the road, all by myself.

On the Road: the classic rite of passage for generations of young men before and after Jack Kerouac. A time of freedom on the roads after leaving school and before the beginning of real life. I would enter it as an aging woman between family life and... what? To find that out, I had to travel by myself because even the most considerate travel companion would derail me from the idea and drown my inner voice which, rather than decide, would keep asking, "are you hungry? You want to stop here? You like this motel? Or should we look for another one?"

Relying completely on myself, taking care of no one else, I would get to know myself all over again.

It was an idea everyone I shared it with, immediately understood and loved, including my publisher and several magazine editors. That was a first. Not that it was my first book. But this was different: Normally I don't know what I'm writing until I see it appear on the page. But this time I had a plan, one I could formulate and sell in thirty seconds. I caught myself talking about it all the time, just because it felt so good to have a plan, an idea everyone understood and found interesting. Maybe I was overdoing it. At some point it began to feel shallow. And the closer the departure came, the less I looked forward to it. Because in the years between coming up with this plan and its execution I had ended my marriage. I lived alone and heard my inner voice speaking louder and quite clear. It said: the last thing I want is to sit alone in a car for days.

Bad timing, you could say. Many would have forced the issue. Not me. To go about it in this way would've meant to ignore precisely what it was all about. More important than the good idea was the question behind it: What do *I* want?

A most radical question for a woman with children. I remember an incident from nearly twenty years earlier. We were in Egypt with friends and the kids, and my younger one was very little and had diarrhea. We thought about leaving for Cairo where another girlfriend was waiting, earlier than planned. I can still see myself sitting on the bed, discouraged, exhausted, in tears.

"What do you want to do?" asked Randa. "Tell me and I'll make it possible."

"Well, for Cyril (my younger son) it would be better... But our friend Ursula had so been looking forward... My mother doesn't want... But Lino (my older son) just said that he wanted..."

Randa shook her head. Then she shook me. "What do YOU want?" she asked. "You, just you!" I looked at her in confusion. "Just me" didn't exist. Couldn't exist. And that was OK. That was how it was supposed to be. Living with young children, having a family and a career is hard enough without having an inner voice crying "and me, and me, and me?" But somewhere along the way that voice was needed again. Turns out it had atrophied, like an unused muscle. In the recent hard years it had been exercised only a little bit. Once in a while I imagined it literally, dangling from the parallel bars, painfully shimmying along like a physiotherapy patient after a serious accident, clumsy but hopeful.

So I sat myself down and tried to listen.

What am I missing?

Not much. Just *Happiness*.

The circumstances of my separation wore me out. My formerly unshakable faith in love was cracked. And my surroundings weren't exactly helping restore it. "That's men for you," women in my age group like to say. "What can you expect?"

Expect? Everything of course! But my inner romantic was fading. Consumptive and wan she lay on a chaise lounge, a lace hanky pressed to her lips. Every separation among my friends, every blind-date horror I learned about, every bitter maxim depleted her more.

Shortly before my departure I knew that there was only one hope for my inner romantic: In order to believe in it again, I had to see happiness with my own eyes. Deliberately I planned my route so I would encounter happy couples on a regular basis. Because they exist. They don't stand out because happiness for them is commonplace. They don't speak of it.

Other than that I'd drift. I'd listen to music, go dancing, do all the things I hadn't done for way too long. Three weeks before departure I realized I had mis-scheduled an appearance. Again, there was the temptation to blow off the whole thing. Adventures are exhausting. Why not simply stay home? Plant my garden, get to know the city I've lived in for two years, make new friends? Swim in the river?

Only, I knew I wouldn't be able to explore the blank space inside if I stayed. However, I did decide to interrupt the trip half way and return to Switzerland for a week or two. I would celebrate my fiftieth in San Francisco where I'd lived for eight years. And in between I'd travel around the country, in search of the unknown.

I was getting excited again. Even more, I set all my hopes on this trip. All my desires. I would throw off the ballast of the past. I would burst free. The happiness of others would rub off on me. I would fall in love en route! Already I saw myself with a garland in my hair standing under a lemon tree marrying a man – faceless so far – and why not? Maybe I wouldn't come back at all...

My fantasy ran away with me before I had reached the airport. Alas, two things right off: It turns out I don't like driving, especially not by myself.

And: Happiness always looks different.

PART ONE:

THE HAPPINESS OF OTHERS

Expressive Dance

My trip begins in New York where I'll spend a few days before visiting my first happy couple. I reach the airport in Zurich at the last minute and on my last legs. At the gate I send off the final column, bent over my computer in concentration. From the corner of my eye I register the movements of other travelers. As long as they are still seated I have time, Time to work. Everyone stands up. I look up and realize I'm at the wrong gate. I catch the flight with minutes to spare. What a beginning! I can't go on like this, I'm thinking.

In the seven years since my return from San Francisco I have turned into a workaholic, completely against my nature. Once a year I fly to the US for a few weeks and always, like now, by the skin of my teeth. I always carry my work with me. Not a single column is skipped. And still, over those few weeks each year, I recover well enough so I can fly home and start all over. While my family and I lived in the states, my day had a simple rhythm, framed by the children's schedules. Once I'd dropped them off at school, the day lie before me. Writing, a yoga class, meeting with friends. Shopping, cooking, cleaning. A simple, predictable life. Every year or two I would publish a new book, then I'd fly to Switzerland for a few weeks and go to Germany for a book tour. When we moved back to Switzerland, everything changed. Intellectually I understood all too well the spiral in which I found myself. From the increasingly painful emptiness of my marriage I escaped into work. At the same time the assignments got more and more interesting and tempting. My sons were growing up fast. I had the freedom to accept more assignments, even travel. How could I say no? The more my private life derailed, the more I buried myself in work. Work became the area in my life where I felt safe. When I write I know what I'm doing. When I lead a seminar I know I have something to give, to pass on. So I kept working more, particularly after the separation.

Where once family life served as a counterweight, holes appeared which I immediately filled with work. I couldn't afford to stop, to think about what was happening. I love my work; I never wanted to do anything other than write. But even work you love can become too much.

In the plane I make lists of things I've been wanting to do for so long. Date. Flirt. Sit in a park, read the newspaper, watch people, drink coffee, talk to friends. Simple things. Daily things. Things I'd forgotten. Lost, maybe.

I'm so tired. But I can't relax, I don't know what to do with my free time. What do I like? What would I like to do? So I do what I know how: I write it down. I make lists.

Dancing is on top. I'd love to dance but I don't dare. Terrible memories of dance lessons when I was young. My ex-husband was the only one who could overlook my absolute inability to be led. In happier days we used to dance in the living room, by the side of the road, in the light of a car beam. That was a long time ago.

I am, there's no other way to say it, a klutz. This unease, this alienation from my own body. There has to be a way out. A writing student tells me about 5 Rhythms, a sort of expressive dance invented in New York. "Everybody moves however they want! Nobody's watching you! You disappear in the crowd, you shake it all off."

That's it! After all, New York is my first stop. That can't be a coincidence. It's a sign!

When I get to New York it's pouring. It's raining so hard traffic stalls. I can't do anything outside. Can't wander the park, sit in the grass, stroll the streets or watch passersby. I didn't expect that. The heavy gray watery curtain drapes itself on my soul. One day passes, then another. I sit in the apartment of my friend Gabriele, I look out the window, I dig through my small suitcase. I brought lovely things, a tight tangerine-colored dress, stilettos, boots with silver rivets, an old fashioned dance dress. Clothes to dance in, to flirt, to be happy in.

When I was training to be a bookseller, the Swiss writer Jürg Federspiel came to our school. He wore a red wool sweater. Back then it was something special that an author would come by to talk to us. And since I already knew that I wanted to be a writer too, I sat in the first row, ready to mimic every word he said. Only, he didn't speak of writing. He told us that in New York a homeless man yelled at him, as though he meant him personally. "Hey you!" he yelled. "Yes, you! Happiness is not the goal!" And that came from an American in America where the right to pursue happiness is written in the constitution. Maybe that's why I kept thinking I'd find happiness "over there." Because there it is my right or even my duty. Or because I have the experiential proof: I was happy there.

Back then during my apprenticeship I didn't understand what Federspiel was trying to tell us. To be honest, I still don't understand. If happiness is not the goal, then what is?

A wild impatience filled me. Let's go! Make the rain quit, the clouds go away. The dark times are past. I want to fall in love, I want to have adventures, I want to laugh! Instead I'm sitting in an apartment and driving myself into despair. I will never be happy, I don't deserve it. It's not part of the plan. My whole life was unplanned. I'm not even supposed to be here!

This kind of despair is my most trusted companion as far back as I remember.

I see, as in an old movie, my young mother sitting on a small hotel bed. The room is shabby, the patterned wallpaper faded. Two narrow beds, separated by a nightstand, bright green duvets. In one bed my father sleeps. He snores. My mother sits with her head sunk to her chest, back bent, hands between her legs. The doctor she'd seen a few times in situations like these doesn't exist anymore. I don't know where this picture comes from. She's never talked to me in detail. But I know exactly how it was, back then in that hotel room. I wasn't but a handful of cells and I remember her despair and mine. I still feel it. Did I have to? Did I really have to be born?

My mother says it was the best thing that could've happened to her. That I was born. I would so love to believe her. But it never feels true. The sense of being a mistake sits deep inside me, as much as the need to undo it. Make it – me – go away. But I don't. I fight. I write. When I write I feel safe. I follow my instinct, an unerring force. As soon as I leave the desk, the certainty is gone.

Gabriele works a lot, we hardly see each other. I tell her about the dance class I signed up for and I can tell she's skeptical. "Can you force yourself to be someone different?" she asks.

"Why someone different? Maybe, in reality, I am someone who dances." And that is exactly how I feel when I walk the busy streets of Soho until I find the dance studio. I climb the stairs, pass an open door past little girls at the barre, pink tutus, leotards. I think of *Fame*. I watched the movie with a girlfriend when I was eighteen. We were both in trade school but neither of us wanted to be a bookseller. We didn't admit that to each other or anyone else. When the film ended we remained in our seats and watched the whole thing again. Afterwards we sat somewhere outside and smoked and were sure we'd succeed. She wanted to be an actor. Me, a writer.

I've only ever wanted to write.

Or, maybe, it was dancing after all?

I am nervous when I enter the studio. A fairy with waist-long hair and a floor-length dress hugs me and starts the music. In between she gives directions I hardly understand, in a hypnotic sing-song. There are few people in the room. I take up more and more space. I feel the tension of the recent months rise up from my feet through my body high into my shoulders and up into my head. I hunch around my own body, around the pain. I shake my head, I throw my arms out. I shake everything off. I dance till I have blisters. After two hours I'm sweaty, exhausted, and – different. Immediately I sign up for the next evening, my last. I cancel the planned dinner with Gabriele. She's happy for me that the dancing helps.

The next evening the class takes place in a bigger room and there are many more people. It's hot, the music is loud, the windows are fogged up. Then we're told to find a partner. "Make eye contact, coordinate your movements!" The next ten minutes we're supposed to dance only with this person, to respond completely to each other. I turn to my right – there's nobody there. I move to the middle of the room, turn around – nobody. I get lost in the crowd, I have dissolved. I don't exist any longer. Five times in a row we're encouraged, five times I remain single. In a hall with hundreds of dancers. Every time I turn toward a person, male or female, young or old, the dancers diverge. The crowd parts like the Red Sea for Moses and I stand in a clearing. In nothingness. The first time I think it's a coincidence. By the second time my familiar companion

'Shame' rises and by the third time I want to jump out a window.

I remember my very first party which we called "Fez." I was in fifth grade. My mother had bought me a long dress and blow-dried my hair. There were eleven girls and ten boys. Two of the boys got in a fist fight so they wouldn't have to dance with me. I sat on a chair all night and told jokes. When I got home, my mother had waited up. I told her it had been amazing. Because I was ashamed. Because I didn't want to disappoint her.

As the dancers turn away from me for the fourth time I leave the room. The first couples are already rolling on the floor. "A safe way to create physical contact," my student called it. "To try it out in a protected space..." Isn't that exactly what I need? Why can't I get that? When I slip into my "lucky boots" my eyes are full of tears. On my way to the subway I feel caught in a bubble in the middle of an empty room. I am separated from all those who sit outside, laugh, eat, talk and kiss. I could sit with them. Eating alone has never bothered me, especially not while traveling. But I've done it all too frequently. I pass by the store fronts, blind to all possibilities. Somewhere I buy a sandwich without checking the filling, and I take the subway home. And there, in the subway, somewhere below the huge city, my despair suddenly lifts. The clouds tear away without warning. I again see the writhing couples on that floor and I start laughing. There's nothing wrong with me. On the contrary, something inside me protects me from the biggest mistakes I could make. The greatest bullshit. Something inside me is healthy and strong: my instinct. I can't wait to tell Gabriele about this but when I get home she's already asleep. I eat my sandwich in the dark. I drink a glass of wine and I think: I'm still here.

The Rowboat: A Dream

Gabriele and I are in a wooden rowboat. The wood is rotten; water comes in through the planks. We row and row and don't advance an inch. Far out a container ship sits, loaded with colorful containers. It doesn't seem to be moving. We row toward it but don't get any closer. Despair fills us, leaks in through crevices like the dirty bay water. Gabriele wants to give up. But there is no quitting: I spy the fin of a shark. I'm gripped by naked panic. The shark circles, dives under the boat. It gets so close I can see its whole huge gray body. It opens its maw: Jaws. Fear of death. A second shark, then a third. Gray fins circle us.

We cry from fear, we know we'll die, we almost wish it were over. And still, we row. We row and row. And then, in one of those time-leaps only possible in dreams, we reach the freighter. A rope ladder hangs from the deck. We escape at the last moment. Below us the boat falls apart and sinks. We hang on the rope ladder above the gaping jaws of the sharks. They can't reach us. We climb up the ladder and pass the meter-high letters of the freighter's name. It's called Heimat, *homeland*.

I'm still laughing when I wake up. Dream interpretation didn't need to have been invented in my case.

The Marriage Vows: Daphne and Paul

The next day I move north, to Maine, where Daphne and Paul run a Mexican restaurant. They are my favorite couple in the world, my touchstone.

Daphne was my first true friend in San Francisco. Emigrating had been a rather unconscious decision; we planned to stay in San Francisco for maybe a year. Which turned into eight. Only once did I question our move, at the very beginning, after we'd been there for a few weeks.

I had already participated in two "play dates" with my then three year old son Cyril. In Zurich kids played together while the mothers sat in kitchens drinking coffee, smoking and talking. But here the mothers, sometimes supported by fathers who take off work, sit on the floors of living rooms with the children, surrounded by mountains of toys, commenting on the slightest twitches: "Samantha, do you want to play with the car? Did you want to show Cyril the car? Cyril, look, Samantha's showing you the car. Great car!! Well done, Samantha. This is fun, isn't it Cyril?"

None of the mothers I met in the nursery school or on the playground seemed to share my need for child-free time, for conversation among adults. They stared at me in surprise when I asked if we should get together without our husbands or kids. "Why?" That was one of the first moments I realized the gulf that separated our culture from America's which, at first sight, had felt so familiar. I had to live in the US for quite some time before I understood what family as opposed to friendship meant.

So I accepted Daphne's invitation to yet another play date with little enthusiasm. Besides, her daughter Lucy was a year older than Cyril and – well – a girl. An hour at the most, I thought as I rang the bell. Daphne opened the door, a bottle of wine and a corkscrew in her hand. "Is it too early for a glass of wine?"

"Oh, God, no!" From relief I almost burst out crying. We stayed the afternoon and then for dinner, even though the children didn't have much in common. But they played contentedly alongside each other while Daphne and I sat on the balcony toasting the thick fog that rolled over the hills like a floating avalanche.

Somewhere along the line she began to cook in a way I hadn't yet seen in America, skillfully yet casually. I think she made pesto. Then her husband Paul came home. He was a musician and a painter, with a pronounced Irish accent. An unassuming man who nonetheless became the center of attention right away. The girls ran toward him, Lucy showed off her new dance steps while Kate showed him a picture she had drawn. Daphne called him "babe."

"How did you two meet?" I ask.

They exchange the kind of look I knew well. "You tell her," Daphne said and turned back to her pesto.

Paul is one of the best story tellers I know, and I know many. Paul and Daphne met in New York, ten -- by now twenty five -- years ago. He was fresh "off the boat" having escaped Northern Ireland in circumstances surrounded by wild rumors. Somewhere between escaping the IRA and an affair turned sour reality probably lay. Paul played in a band and while he was waiting for the breakthrough, he was bussing tables in a restaurant where a beautiful waitress rejected his advances almost daily. Daphne, like so many women, had a weakness for "bad boys," men who make her cry. Like that day when Paul found her wiping her eyes.

"Now you have to go out with me tonight," he said with the courage of the desperate. "Come out with me and make both our days better!" It wasn't a question, since he'd asked so often. But this day could only get better so she shrugged and said, yes. Or, rather: Why not?

He waited for her shift to be over. They went here and there and then he went home with her. Where he still is. Three weeks after that first night she was pregnant. They raised two daughters and went hand in hand across the red carpet as his band was nominated for a Grammy. They ran a successful breakfast restaurant they named after their oldest daughter and which appeared in travel guides as "the best that Haight Ashbury produced in the Summer of Love!" *Kate's Kitchen* is also the place where Piper Kerman, the author of *Orange is the New Black,* met her husband. At least that's what a newspaper reported recently.

Back then, when I met them in San Francisco, Paul had started working as a painter. I hired him to paint my house a specific shade of raspberry red. Patiently he looked at crushed berries and spoonfuls of sorbet, trying to figure out exactly what I wanted. Daphne called every day around noon. By the third day I understood that she wasn't calling for me but for him.

"I'll go home for a short while," he said. When he returned after a few hours he sang one of his old songs while working.

"Paul is a lucky devil," his apprentice, another Irishman, said with longing.

A few years later, after the dot-com wave hit the bay area, Daphne and Paul like so many others, looked for a cheaper place to live. They packed their car and took off. All the way across the country to the east coast. To a brother who ran a construction company. But, contrary to promises, he didn't have a job for Paul. So there they sat, four people in a shabby apartment in a place they knew no one and where there was no work. The kids had already been enrolled in school. They were stuck. The east coast winter was endless, dark and icy cold.

I remember the phone conversations we had. I remember Daphne's bravery. Was the biggest decision of her life a mistake? No. The biggest decision had been to go out on that first date with Paul. And they were still together. They might stumble over the life set out for them, but not over each other. After eight months Daphne's twin sister Eloise called. She was a talented chef with whom they'd run *Kate's Kitchen* back in San Francisco. Eloise had bought a dilapidated restaurant in Maine, two states north up the coast, and asked if they wanted to join her.

Now I'm sitting in their small house in Brunswick, Maine, right next to the restaurant *El Camino*, the only Mexican restaurant in the state. It's going well, the kitchen has been written up in several magazines. Daphne spends the mornings shopping and doing prep work, her sister cooks, Paul receives the guests – but not today. Today the restaurant is closed. So Daphne cooks. She makes pesto, like back when we first met.

"Do you remember?" I ask.

"Oh, God, yes!" she laughs. "You remember how my mother called? 'Daphne what are you cooking? Uh... noodles and pesto... Good. But you made the pesto from scratch? And the basil is homegrown? Good, but what about the olive oil? Did you press it yourself?'"

We laugh. In the eyes of her mother, Daphne is the black sheep of the family. Because she's not "creative," she doesn't paint, her furniture and clothes are not handmade, she doesn't use makeup. Because she never wanted anything other than a happy family life, a welcoming home, a table where people would gather. How many evenings have I spent like this, sitting at her kitchen table, watching her work effortlessly, listening to Paul's stories?

One evening we lounge on the sofa and I talk about my unpleasant divorce. "Did I ever tell you about my first divorce?" Paul asks. I grin. "My first divorce." The perfect title for a born story-teller. Even though his first divorce was his only one. I know the story. It ends with the money-grabbing ex-wife settling for a pair of genuine American Levi jeans. "My mother's divorce was worse," Paul continues. "My father left for America, with money borrowed from a nun, to make his fortune. We were supposed to follow. "Give me three months, he said, to build something. At most, six." But we didn't hear from him for four years. He finally wrote to my mother. He wanted to talk about everything, wanted to know if she could forgive him, asked her to come to New York. My mother pondered for days and endured sleepless nights. What should she do, where would the money for a ticket come from? She still loved her husband. The neighbors all chipped in. Finally she got on a plane. When he picked her up in New York, my father said "Surprise! We're heading to Reno where we can get a cheap divorce."

"Oh, but then she met the race car driver, tell that one!" Daphne begs. "You remember him, the one with the ponies!" This lover promised Paul's mother he'd marry her. He would build a house for her and the four children, with a barn for four ponies. One for each child. Paul and the siblings had already named the ponies. Finally everything would turn out well. Paul's mother Pat gave notice at her job and canceled the flat. At the arranged time they stood by the side of the road with their suitcases and waited for the race car driver. It turned out he did build a house and a barn and had bought ponies. Only, unfortunately, for a different woman and different children.

"You really should write these stories down," I say, not for the first time. "If you don't, I will!"

The fridge holds an invitation to a wedding. On it a photo of a windblown middle aged couple in love. "Who are they?" I ask, holding the picture.

"That's Jenny, our waitress... She lived in the apartment below us for a while. And Dave was one of our regulars. When he first came to the *El Camino* it was with his wife. The marriage was difficult. "They fought a lot in the restaurant," Paul remembers. He also claims to know exactly when Dave fell in love with the waitress. But it was another eighteen months until he got out of his marriage and divorced. Only then did he speak to Jenny.

My jaw drops. That exists for real? I have to tell this to my bitter girlfriends! So much for "all men lie, all men cheat!" Jenny wasn't easily swayed at first. It took at least another three months until she agreed to a date. After that, things moved fast.

"I remember sitting in her flat and looking around," Paul continues. "Everything was jam packed with furniture, clutter, memories. 'Jenny' I said, 'how do you figure a man could fit here?' She cleaned out her apartment and then..."

Is my life too full? I wonder. In Lucy's room where I sleep, the walls are painted blue. During an adolescent crisis she drew maxims on the walls in intricate cursive script. "Be soft. Do not let the world make you hard. Do not let the pain make you hate. Do not let bitterness steal your sweetness..." They seem strangely fitting and comforting to me now. I won't tell her, though. Lucy should still believe that life will become easier. That adults have a grip on it. I think I was forty before I gave up the hope that one day everything would be clear, everything would make sense. That I would know what I was doing and why.

Daphne and I take a day trip up the coast. Daphne drives my rental, as she's a bad passenger. We listen to a CD Paul gave me. Quietly and in private he's begun to make music again. Patiently he records all the tracks, one after the other, in the small room where the washing machine is. He posts the songs and they travel through Facebook; two have become the soundtracks of independent films. The red carpet is being rolled out again for Paul and Daphne but it has a different meaning from twenty years ago.

We stop by the ocean, it's cool and I think of all the summer clothes in my suitcase. We eat lobster rolls, yummy and cheap. I'm thrilled. Lobster is a treat I can hardly ever afford in Switzerland. Daphne is baffled. "Here, lobster is nothing special" she says "they throw this stuff at you and after a while you're sick of it."

All a question of perspective.

Later Paul says, "women like you and Daphne don't have it easy. You're so beautiful and strong you can scare a man."

Daphne frowns. "Beautiful and strong, me?" In the last five years they have both had cancer, first he, then she. After the treatment, Daphne no longer looks in the mirror. She doesn't recognize herself. Clearly it's not enough to be desired in order to feel desirable. She looks at him, he grins, "fortunately I don't get scared easily." She smiles. The next day she moves the marital bed into another room, one "in which I was not ill." I don't think life has dealt gently with Daphne and Paul. But they are all the more so with each other. Their bond is as solid and unassuming as they are. They embody the classic marital vows like no other couple I know. "For better or worse, for richer or poorer, in sickness and in health…" Obviously I have wrongly raised my inner romantic on French movies and Russian novels, leading her to believe that only relationships full of drama could be real. But life is drama enough, why lacerate each other as well?

"You teach people how to treat you," Daphne says. "The way they treat you is the way you taught them." I know that already! That's why it doesn't help me to badmouth my ex-husband, even if sometimes it feels good. The question isn't "what did he do?" The question for me is: Why did I participate?

I know the answer to that. I have trained myself not to trust my instincts, not to listen to my own concerns because the alternative, to question the person I loved, was intolerable. I cannot blame anyone for that, not even myself. I know everything I need to know. I am facing my demons. I don't hide. I look at them closely, I work on myself. But it's hard. I'm so tired. I would just like to have a good time for once. Is that too much to ask?

.

The Advantages of Traveling Solo

Very early in the morning I sneak out of the sleeping house and take my rental back to Portland International Jetport. Once there I realize I don't have my passport. I call Daphne. She turns the house upside down – nothing.

A driver's license, the universal ID in the US, should be good enough for a national flight, she thinks.

More than twenty years before I had once already visited New Orleans, my next stop. We were four adults in a rented house and nobody had a driver's license. We explored the city on rented bikes. Whenever we needed to exchange money, long before e-banking and ATMs, we proudly handed over our Swiss passports. They were turned this way and that, with suspicion. "Don't you have a driver's license?" – "Sorry, no." Today it's the other way around. The driver's license doesn't help, they want to see the red passport.

Since September 11, 2001, – "9/11, you know?" – foreigners are only allowed to fly with valid passports, even on domestic flights. "We really aren't allowed to let you fly at all." But the "really" leaves a bit of leeway to be explored. While I wait a strange sense of peace fills me. What's the worst that can happen? I miss a flight to New York, the train to New Orleans? So what? I'll simply call Daphne and she'll come to pick me up. We'll drive back to Brunswick. I'll spend the rest of my time in one place, why not? Didn't Paul say, stay with us, stay in Maine, we'll find you a man? By now I am almost hoping for this outcome. But before I can let fate take over, they wave me through. My hand luggage is searched a second time, I am patted down thoroughly, and then I sit on the plane to New York.

That which could've taken on the dimensions of a catastrophe is no problem at all: because I'm traveling solo. Only *I* suffer from my mistakes – if at all – and no one else is responsible. No one can make me feel bad about it – and I have no one else to blame. I fly to New York, take a taxi to the Swiss Consulate and have them issue an emergency passport. I continue on to the train station in the taxi. In the meantime rush hour has set in. I get out early and make the final hundred yards on foot, my hair flies, my shawl unwinds, how many movies have I seen this in? Now time is short. I can't find the right platform. I don't understand that I have to take the escalator. But the *Southern Crescent* is waiting for me. An impatient red light blinks, a heavyset conductor gestures and blows her whistle. I run along the empty platform dragging the suitcase, my shawl falls to the floor.

The trip takes thirty-one hours. For thirty-one hours I'm neither here nor there. I reserved a sleeper compartment, two beds and a toilet, all to myself. Four meals included. I didn't expect much, what do Americans know about train rides, I think. Typical Swiss arrogance. For the money this luxurious compartment costs, Daphne and Paul, when they come to visit me the following year, can barely pay for tickets from Aarau to Luzern. I settle myself in like in a hotel room. Take pictures through the window. The conductor introduces herself by name, "I am Roslyn. Man, you sure cut it close! Welcome to the Crescent." As soon as she's gone, someone else knocks at the door. A woman with bleached blond hair that looks like a wig, "I'm Debbie, your Conductor. If you need anything at all, let me know." I'm speechless. Later, Debbie knocks at the door, "Dinner is served." It's five in the afternoon.

"OK," I yell back. "Thanks"

When I get to the dining car an hour later, Debbie stops me. "Honey, there you are! I was worried."

"Worried?"

"I called and knocked, didn't you hear me?"

"Yes, and I responded."

"Yeah, but then you didn't come to dinner." She shakes her head, then lets me go. I am strangely touched. Someone's keeping an eye on me. I am alone but not alone. I am safe in a train, regarded, noticed. It matters whether I come to dinner or not.

I am shown to a table for eight where the first service has already ended and the second begins. Two sisters sit near me, one from the Carolinas, the other from California. Once a year they go to a family reunion, always by train. "You never have so much time to catch up!" "And you can't avoid each other!" The two sisters are near clichés of the extremes of typical American women. Carol, a Southern belle with a perfectly coiffed hairdo, immaculately white sneakers, polite to a fault and if one didn't know any better it might be taken as a spoof. Andrea, no makeup, gray haired, a quintessential Northern Californian intellectual, orders a salad without dressing, a veggie burger, and a whiskey. Carol encircles me with careful questions until she finds a neutral conversation topic. Andrea, on the other hand, puts her finger directly on the sore points. "Why are you traveling alone? Don't you have any friends?" My marital status her sister Carol has already squeezed out. "Or maybe a girlfriend?" Before I can answer, Carol jumps in, steering the conversation to sager topics again. "How do you like the landscape here? Switzerland is supposed to be beautiful. But look outside, see those trees!" Which one of the two is the typical American? And am I a typical Swiss? Will they say from now on that the Swiss prefer to travel alone, that they divorce frequently, that they lack concrete plans?

The sisters say goodbye. I sit alone at the table, waiting for my food. If this were a movie, a good-looking dark stranger would now sit down. And that's exactly what happens. Only, Tom is married. And in his nineties. He had just become a great-grandfather and is taking the train from Baltimore to Charlottesville. He recently turned in his driver's license, with reluctance. He shows me pictures of his great-grandson, actual photos he pulls from his wallet, not cell phone shots.

I order a steak, it's surprisingly good. I can't remember having eaten so well on European trains. And it's included, no matter what it costs, the steak for twenty dollars or the burger for twelve. Only the wine is extra, "Sorry, ma'am."

When I return to my compartment, both beds have been made up. Did Debbie make provisions in case I met someone in the dining car? Or did she simply want to give me the choice? Whatever. The gesture moves me. I honor it by using both beds. Every time I wake up, I climb up or down the stepladder. Outside the night passes by.

Leave It with Miss Gypsy

In New Orleans, where I had planned to stay for three days, my absurd achievement ambition catches up with me. The quiet days with Daphne and Paul had been wonderful, but now! Now it's time to fast forward, to hurry up, to be happy! Go out, listen to music, dance, flirt! Let's go! I don't have all the time in the world, after all.

But the in-law unit behind Jack and Mike's house – another happy couple whom I don't know and only meet by chance on Airbnb – is dark and stuffy, hard to air out. The furnishings are plush, dark, satin and velvet. I don't do well in the heat, the humidity. My feet swell. I buy a bottle of wine, turn on the AC and the TV. Reality shows play on all the channels. Twelve men woo one woman, twelve women woo one man. It's always the same. I'm not alone, we all want the same thing. I change channels. Teens escape the Amish community and get drunk in the big city. Click. Brides lose their nerve, toss bouquets, screech. Click. Amish teens attempt to deal with issues they are not familiar with, like cars, TV, alcohol. Click. A medium with dangerous looking artificial nails goes to a fitness center where she starts receiving messages from the personal trainer's dead mother. The hulky man dissolves in tears. Here I get stuck. I wish someone would tell me what comes next. What I should do. After all, I have a mission. I have to recover, I have to be happy, and where in this dark, dank city will I find happiness? I consult my list. Dancing, that's still on top. And I'm in New Orleans where every other building is a club and where they even play music in the street. And dance. I turn off the TV, throw on a dress. I go outside, along the road, I hear music coming from everywhere. The sounds mingle. Again and again I

23

stop, peer in, can't decide. I disappear in the crowd, I dissolve. In the end, without knowing how, I land in the one empty place without music. I order a glass of wine, leave without drinking it, slide a twenty dollar bill under the glass, way too much. On the way home I get lost, all the street names sound the same. It's still hot.

I am ashamed. Again, I failed.

The next day I roam the streets and keep ending up at the same place. Twice I pass a Voodoo shop, the second time I enter noticing that priestess Madame Denise offers personal consultations. I spontaneously decide to ask if she has time and get an appointment in half an hour. The shop is small but air conditioned. I would love to stay here. But I'm afraid to interfere with the consultation taking place in a corner. The curtain doesn't close all the way. I see a couple close together on a chair, the girl half on his lap. I can't hear what Madame Denise is saying but I hear the customer laughing, too loud.

I step outside, the heat slaps my face. I fight my way a few yards down the road to another air conditioned store where I study every single post card. Suddenly I recall a winter in New York where Cyril and I hastened from one store to the next. We held our breath till we were inside. It was the cold, the relentless wind that hurt our lungs. I yearn for the temperate climate of San Francisco. In all my years there I didn't even own a winter coat. But no bathing suit, either.

The minutes pass slowly; time seems to melt into the wet heat. I return to the Voodoo shop. I have to wait. Finally the curtain moves and the couple emerges. She thanks the Madame and buys some candles. Of course, I think, a tourist trap. Madame Denise will tell me, too, which herbs and candles and Gris-Gris I need to buy, all available right there. How convenient. I remember the medium from New Jersey and think I might as well go home and watch TV. But I had paid in advance. And now Madame Denise gestures to me. She appears tired, listless, maybe stoned. She smokes. No, she doesn't smoke but an ashtray and lighter are ready on the table next to a deck of cards. She closes her eyes. Then she looks at me.

"Giiiirrrllll, you are so tired!" she cries out.

"Well, yeah..." I'm a bit offended, after all I've been away for ten days already, I shouldn't be so tired, I shouldn't look so tired. "You're tired," she repeats. "Tired, tired, tired! Tired of always being there for others, doing for others. Tired. Just exhausted."

She speaks of the place where I'm living, that I'm looking for a new one, that I want to work less, retire. "For you, it's all about retirement." What does she mean by that? Should I stop working? The mere mention fills me with panic. Work is all I have left. But the word also means retreat. Retreat to where?

"To San Francisco?" I say hopefully.

"Giirrrlllll I loooooove Frisco!" But, no, she doesn't see San Francisco, it's another place she can't name, for sure it's not New York or Los Angeles. "A place where you can write well... your sons will help you..." I hadn't mentioned my sons. Suddenly she hesitates, stops short. "Who tried to put a curse on you?" she asks.

Put a curse on me? I don't understand.

"You know someone from here, from Louisiana?" she asks. "Someone who knows Voodoo? Or maybe someone from Haiti?"

My breath catches in my throat. How the hell did she get on to Haiti? I haven't told her anything about the end of my marriage, or the role a young woman from Haiti played in it. That's all done and dusted. I'm here for something else, I'm looking for happiness. I want to hear of new places, of a good looking dark stranger who will enter my life. I want to look forward, not back. Madame Denise is still waiting for an answer.

"Well, yeah," I say weakly. "But I only met her once and she was totally nice to me."

"Nice!" Madame Denise snorts. "Do you have something this person wants for herself?"

"No," I say sharply "I don't." I can't believe it. I refuse to believe it. Suddenly I remember my ex-husband returning from one of his earlier trips to Haiti with an empty bottle of rum, decorated with cloth and beads that he had received from a Voodoo priest. "I caught your soul inside it," he said. At the time, I found it romantic.

"The curse didn't really catch," Madame Denise reassures me. "But it does explain why you're so tired."

"What do I have to do?"

"Nothing. Just be yourself." She hugs me for a long time. "Thank you," she says. "Thank you for your soul and your spirit."

She didn't do that with the earlier customers. I am touched. She doesn't try to sell me anything either, no candles, no Gris-Gris, nothing. She just gives me a business card and recommends a Reiki treatment.

The Reiki practitioner is called Miss Gypsy. She's surprised when I call and say "Madame Denise sent me."

"Madame Denise? What an honor. I didn't know she had my business cards." I can see her the same afternoon. Still, I feel I should experience something of the city. I try to remember back twenty five years. What did we do? I suddenly remember we took a river boat on the Mississippi. My friend carried Lino, my then two-year old son into the engine room and explained with great seriousness and exactitude how a paddle steamer worked. I remember how I laughed. "How is a two-year-old supposed to understand? I don't even understand it."

But afterwards Lino always wanted to take the steam boat in Zurich, the "Dampfrater" he called it, instead of "Raddampfer". I go down to the river and there it is, the Dampfrater. The *Natchez*. It looks exactly the same as twenty-five years before. The horn blows for departure and, without hesitation, I buy a ticket. I sit in the stern, look down at the wheel, the red paddles that turn and turn. They lift the brown water and let it fall. I still don't understand how it works. But I don't go down into the engine room; I simply watch the water being churned by the red paddles. For these two hours I don't have to do anything. I don't have to experience anything. I don't have to check anything off my list. I don't have to be happy.

Miss Gypsy's office is in the same quarter where I'm staying. I walk there, my soles burn, the thin sandals can't keep out the heat from the asphalt. I escape into the air-conditioned alternative shopping center. Downstairs there is a health food store and a bookstore, upstairs are the offices. *Affordable Healing Arts*. Affordable is right. The ninety minute session costs only sixty dollars. I offer to pay more, a tourist tariff, I know I'm more well-off than the locals. I wouldn't want to exploit a deal which was not meant for me. Suddenly I recall a fight I had with my ex-husband. We were in Cairo getting out of a taxi, where he argued with the driver. He refused to pay the tourist fare. "We are not tourists," he said "we work here." I was embarrassed. "Yes, but we're paid in Switzerland, in Swiss Francs!" I was ashamed. I handed the driver the rest of the fare, my husband was irritated; the scene repeated itself in other places.

Why do I remember just now? I shake my head to dislodge the memory. That's over, I remind myself. You're over it! My mantra. The office help sends me into the treatment room. Miss

Gypsy looks like an aged Juliette Greco, black haired with heavy mascara, a facelift and breast implants. When I enter tears come to her eyes. What a beginning, I think.

"Ah, Milena," she says. She pronounces my name correctly, Milena. Not Miliina or M'leina. She pronounces my name as if she knew me. Even more, as if I meant something to her. Her voice is so full of sympathy that I nearly start crying. After all, on this trip I usually talk to myself. And my tone is anything but sympathetic. I'm suddenly aware of how much pressure I've been putting on myself. Do something! Relax! Be happy! Go dancing! Fall in love, don't remain alone. What would people think? What if they think you're not normal? Because, really, I lost the camouflage my marriage provided. At least in the final, bourgeois phase. Nobody could tell we were unhappy. We appeared like a regular family, in a nice house with a nice garden and a big car in the driveway. Someone with all that had to be normal. Couldn't be crazy.

My knees buckle, I sink down into the single chair. Miss Gypsy watches me. Her gaze is... I can't quite name it... a mixture of love and concern... motherly! That's it. With motherly concern she shakes her head. "You carry so much with you," she says. "Put it down. Leave it here." It's my first Reiki treatment. I feel touches where there aren't any, I blink, I suddenly feel her hands on my feet even though she's standing behind me, by my head. My stomach cramps. I feel nauseous, then it passes. After the session she describes her impressions: in her mind, she saw me vehemently toss items into a trash can.

Good, I think. Exactly!

Then she described an animal with horns, a ram or wild goat that repeatedly rammed his horns into my center, who wouldn't leave me alone, who destroyed my life energy. "His name starts with a T," she says. "Could he be from Egypt?"

My ex-husband whom I met in Egypt, astrological sign Aries, first name begins with T…

I begin to cry. I'm so tired of it all. It's been so long. I don't want to have to deal with it any longer, I want to leave it all behind, I want to look into the future. Why does all this old garbage still cling to me?

"Leave it here," Miss Gypsy repeats. "Leave it with Miss Gypsy."

She, too, hugs me on the way out.

That evening I don't go out either. I am knocked out. I buy ten books and strange precooked food, advertised as healthy. I wonder what my landlords think seeing the light on in the bungalow, if they're curious why I'm not going out, here in New Orleans, in the hip new quarter where at every corner bars and clubs spring up, where all the youth hostels and backpacker spots are located. I haven't done anything on my list. Nothing I imagined. I often think of my sons and how they'd like it here. Not me. This place is not for me. But at least I know why I had to come here: to leave everything with Miss Gypsy.

Hugging Alligators: Susanne and Doug

"What do you want to do in Breaux Bridge – hug alligators?" the taxi driver asks on the way to the airport where I'm supposed to pick up my rental car. The airport is fifteen miles in the opposite direction of my destination in Southern Louisiana. Again I'm not very well organized. Even more so when I find myself at the counter realizing I had reserved the car for the following day. Typical, I think. Again, I'm happy I'm traveling solo. No one gets irritated with me. Not even myself. I am a catastrophic traveler. As a younger woman I was too vein to wear glasses and kept getting on the wrong trains. Basel instead of Baden, Amsterdam instead of Zurich. Once I got off a train only at the switchyard and walked along the tracks back to the train station in Milan. When I finally discovered contact lenses, things didn't improve. Hardly a trip goes by without incident. Forgotten passport, wrong day at the airport, expired passport, missed plane, and I still always end up on the wrong train. But that's not the worst: the worst is the panic that rises in me, an immeasurable despair over my absolute inability to conquer the simplest everyday tasks.

On this trip I finally realize: it doesn't matter at all. Nothing can happen. So I stand here and chat with Kasha at the counter until a different car is found, an even better one. As soon as this problem is solved another one pops up: none of my credit cards work. A call to Switzerland reveals that my credit card bills had been returned as undeliverable. All I had done was put a vacation hold on my mail. Decide! It seems the post office is saying. We no longer tolerate this back and forth between two continents. Either you stay here or you don't exist! We erase you!

An hour later, Kasha and I have exchanged half our life stories, admired pictures of our children, and have ensured each other that we could handle whatever life might throw our way. I manage to make my presence in Switzerland credible, to reactivate my credit cards, and Kasha hands me a key to a car with AC. The ten mile drive back in the direction I just came from doesn't bother me any longer. I have learned one thing: on a trip nothing, apart from a real catastrophe, can go wrong. Everything is an adventure. Everything is an experience. The pictures of Kasha's children are just as interesting as a visit to a museum.

I turn up the radio and drive down the straight highway to Southern Louisiana where Susanne and Doug live.

Susanne was my first editor at the legendary Kroesus Publishing House. For six years I sent out my manuscripts and for six years I got nothing but rejections. Mostly form letters, always the same. " ... regret to have to inform you... doesn't fit our profile..." If anyone ever took time for a personal answer, it always sounded the same. "You have no talent, you can't write, you'll never publish a book." Only one, I think he was an editor with Rowohlt, a publisher I ended up with later, wrote he hardly ever laughed as much as when he read my stories, but still "this is not literature. This cannot be published." Why didn't I give up? I don't know. It cannot be because of an overwhelming self confidence. I never knew whether I was good or not. I only knew: this is it. This is what I do. I am someone who writes. So I took temp jobs here and there and kept writing. And somewhere along the line, some friends decided, enough with all the unsuccessful efforts and they founded a publishing house, the aforementioned Kroesus Verlag. Even the *Putzfraueninsel*, to date my most well-known book, would not have been printed without Kroesus Verlag. I now remember that I was in New Orleans the first time shortly after my first book, *Gebrochene Herzen,* had been published. Back then I had my cards read on Jackson Square. "Will my book be a great success?" I asked. The reader shrugged and said, "not so much. But the second one, that will be an international best seller!" As I said that was the *Putzraueninsel.* Susanne edited it.

Which meant I'd known Susanne for twenty-five years but hadn't seen her for about twenty. Until a birthday party in Zurich six months earlier. When she told me she was in the process of emigrating to Louisiana.

"I want to take a road trip next year," I said. "Maybe I'll check out your corner of the country?"

"Absolutely," she said. "For sure you have to come see us." I remember thinking: she already sounds so American. As I stood at her door a year later, Switzerland caught up with me. Suddenly I wondered if this is such a good idea, we don't really know each other any longer, she's recently married, I don't want to be a burden, what if we have nothing to say to each other? To be on the safe side I had invited myself for only three days. For three days, everyone knows, fish stay fresh in the fridge and guests are tolerable.

A half hour later the inner Swiss has disappeared. We sit on the veranda, drink beer, talk, don't talk, look out across the land. It appears to me an endless expanse.

"Come on, I'll show it to you before the sun goes down. Susanne walks ahead of me through the knee-high grass. "Should mow this," she says and grins. "It's my absolutely favorite thing to do here: putter about with the lawn mower."

We pace off the land – a grandiose expression but it fits here. Susanne knows every blade of grass, every rock. I have never seen such a landscape; it's endearing and primordial at the same time. As if at any moment dinosaurs could stomp through the high grass. If we turned away for an instant nature would erase any trace of our presence behind our backs. Everything grows greener here, more lush and more dense than anywhere else. The insects are bigger, the flower buds too. Crickets chirp, someone practices violin, somewhere a dog barks. Slowly the sky turns pink, even those colors are more intense, richer.

A neighbor meets us. Susanne chats with her, asks about her husband. Her English has already assumed the soft local cadence and she sprinkles her sentences with Creole terms of endearment "cher" - darling.

I don't know the last time I had seen anyone so clearly in the right place as was Susanne. She belongs here. Not the US, not the Southern states, not New Orleans, no, specifically here, this spot, in Southern Louisiana, Cajun country. What is it? The land, the people, the music? All of the above?

"It's completely un-American," she says. It's what we Europeans always say when we particularly like a place in the US. "It's so European, so un-American." As if justifying that America is simply different than what we thought. America is everything and the opposite of it all. Actually, America is what we didn't imagine. Like this old-fashioned politeness that is normal in Southern Louisiana. And which lends itself to a particular elegance of daily life, a life which for most of the residents is not exactly easy.

We return to the house and settle in again on the veranda for the most breathtaking of imaginable sunsets. Their home is wonderful, an old pale-blue sharecropper house they renovated themselves. "Yesterday the bedroom got finished," Susanne says, "so you can have the guest bedroom." At the moment the rear veranda is under construction. When I get up in the morning, my breakfast sits ready, homemade bread, honey, coffee. The bread is absolutely delicious. You can't buy anything like it here, Susanne comments with an ironic undertone poking fun at a health-conscious American who asked her suspiciously if she'd added gluten.

It's hot and humid but less oppressive than New Orleans. The rhythm of life is slower. We sit on the veranda, friends come by, take a seat, everyone makes plans for later, the evening, the weekend. At some point you get up, grab a brush or a hammer and keep working.

"We could open a burn-out clinic," Doug says. "The Breaux-Bridge-Slow-Down-Program!" Everybody who comes here relaxes. You can't rush in this heat. Susanne didn't rush. She waited for the right moment. For twenty years she's known she wanted to live here. Every year she came here to improve her fiddle playing. I didn't even know she played the Cajun fiddle – and very well. Even less did I know what making music meant here. She met Doug in a music workshop. During their first meeting they "started a conversation that hasn't ended yet." For two years they had a long distance relationship until they turned her old dream, to leave cold, gray and rhythm-starved Switzerland, for life in Louisiana into reality. And the perfect house materialized. An affordable fixer-upper, a rare jewel. Most of the old sharecropper homes have long been torn down or remodeled until the simple, traditional lines are destroyed. This house kept its clear lines while waiting for Doug and Susanne. Proudly it stands between two mobile homes like an aging dancer between overweight teenagers. The right house at the right place with the right man. Ten years earlier or a year later and everything would've been different.

When is the right moment? After my marriage ended I often regretted my decision to return to Switzerland. Not because I don't like Switzerland but because I did well in San Francisco. I was home there. Only I wanted to keep the family together. I wanted to remain married. The move could save a crumbling relationship, so I thought. I should've known better.

It doesn't help to look back and rearrange the past like the furniture of a doll house – and still I couldn't stop myself those first months after the separation. I thought: if I'd stayed, what could have been avoided. 'What if...' is a good beginning for a story: for life, it's useless. And now that I look at Susanne, knee-deep in grass, one hand on her hip, the other shading her eyes from the sun, inspecting her land and her house, deciding at this very moment to mow the lawn – now, for the first time I realize: it'll all make sense.

Susanne likes to describe herself as the "most unromantic woman in the world." She prefers wearing paint spattered overalls and is most content when she drives across the field on her power mower. Or, when she makes music. Since she moved here she plays the fiddle daily and goes dancing every other night. At first I don't understand how this works. "Do you have a concert tomorrow?" I ask. She shrugs her shoulders, "We'll see what's up." There's always music somewhere. In the afternoon when the friends gather on the veranda, plans for the evening get aired. "Who's on today at the Cafe des Artistes?" "Anyone going to Lafayette?"

You just tuck your instrument under your arm and drive there, listen, join in. Chairs are set in a half circle, sometimes there are more musicians on stage than an audience before it. Often they exchange roles. After two days I recognize many of the faces. People move here from all over, for the love of music. And so it's always the first question I am asked, "what instrument do you play?"

"The pen," I say. I try to imagine a place where writers could meet so casually, talk, collaborate. I would move there instantly.

During a birthday party I sit with some old ladies at the edge of the dance floor. Susanne gets ready to play. "Look at those old couples," Susanne says to me. "Those who regularly dance together stay in love." And already she's organized a charming dance partner for me. But I don't know the steps, I am clumsy, I stiffen up. Even when Juan, a complete gentleman, thanks me for each dance with a bow, I am embarrassed.

I see what Susanne means. But I feel excluded. I should take dance lessons. I should wear flat shoes. I should, I should...

Juan reappears and asks me to dance. "This is a waltz, you know that one!"After I get back to my chair an old, red-faced man, grabs my arm and grins, "well, you can lead the boots to the dance floor but you can't make them dance."

The next day when we get ready to go out again, Susanne sits on the floor polishing her dance boots. She is completely absorbed. Her back is bent, hair hangs over her face and covers her fairytale blue eyes. Doug, who was about to show me his boots, goes silent in the middle of his sentence, gets lost looking at her. An old envy rises in me: why doesn't anyone look at me that way? Why am I never good enough? Why doesn't anybody love me the way I am? "I never felt I got first prize with you," my ex-husband once said. I shake off the memory. What did Daphne say? "You teach people how to treat you."

On my last day we wander along the meandering shores of Lake Martin. Directly in front of us an alligator glides into the water, dives, resurfaces. Blinking those motionless eyes. Strangely enough I'm not afraid. In this lake there aren't only alligators. There are also herons nesting. Hundreds, maybe thousands. I have never seen this many herons. And I know: if you see a heron you make a wish. And so I wish and wish and wish until I'm empty. Completely wished out.

In the early evening I drive the thirty mile long Atchafalaya Basin Bridge back toward New Orleans. The basin is a primordial endless water landscape. The crowns of trees emerge from the dark green water like tiny islands. It feels as though I'm heading directly for the swamp. The safety rail seems extremely low. My hands cramp around the wheel. I see myself falling off the bridge, sinking into the water, being eaten by alligators. Having a strong imagination is not always and in every instant advantageous. I keep my eyes stiffly in front. "The wheel follows the eyes," Judy, my driving instructor from Fearless Driving, used to say. I only learned to drive at thirty-six, because I had to living in San Francisco. Back then I refused to use the freeway or go across bridges, which restricted my mobility quite seriously in a city surrounded by water on three sides. And now I'm driving across a swamp bridge as if it were nothing! Well, nearly.

I've come far. In all respects. Suddenly I relax. On the radio they play Oldies. I turn it up and begin to sing along. I believe I finally understand: it's not a question of finding a man who loves me the way I am. Who doesn't ask me to bend. It's about me not bending, that I am the way I am, that I like myself. And as if on cue, a young Sinead O'Connor splits the air with "Nothing compares 2U..." She's right, I think and sing loudly along with her. And suddenly my inner romantic agrees and I'm simply happy. All by my lonesome.

The Curse of San Francisco

On the plane to Dallas I sit next to a Swiss couple continuing on to San Francisco. A strong yearning for my city fills me. It'll be awhile before I get to see 'her' again. Simultaneously this longing has something nostalgic as if San Francisco weren't my future but my past.

As we returned to Switzerland after eight years in The City, everybody except for me was sure that the San Francisco chapter was closed. It was fun, thanks, goodbye. My little house on top of the hill should be sold, my debts paid off, maybe I'd have something left over. My then husband wanted a vacation home in Ireland. I remained uncompromising. Against all reason I held onto the house. It had been my home. One day I wanted to return there. At least part time.

For years it seemed the others would be proven right, those who said: "What do you want with this house? What's up with that? It's just a hassle!" Yet it started out so well. Shortly before our departure I found out that a family, connected to us through Cyril's school, desperately needed a house. Sigal, the mother, an Israeli artist with intense blue eyes, came in through the front door, looked around, nodded and said, "We'll take it." Before she'd seen more than the entrance.

"Don't you want to look around?"

She shook her head. "Not necessary. I love your house so much I'd love to strap it to my back and take it with me everywhere," she said. That was exactly the way I had reacted when I entered my house the first time. I hugged her and that was it. But just a year later they decided to leave, to go back to New York. I needed to find new renters. Cyril and I wanted to spend the summer in San Francisco. He wanted to visit his friends, and I could deal with the house that now stood empty apart from a bed a friend had built for me to fit precisely under the sloping roof. "You won't be able to put that bed anywhere else," he'd said. And I, "why would I? I'll never live anywhere else."

"You want to make God laugh," says my favorite proverb, "tell Her your plans." I borrowed some bed linens, towels, dishes. Actually I was thinking of furnishing it and renting it out by the month, returning twice a year with my sons. Later they would move in on their own, with their friends and girlfriends. A vacation home, only at the other end of the world. But that turned out to be too complicated. Who would look after the constantly changing renters? Besides, at that point, my daily life revolved around school schedules. There was no time but a few weeks in summer. So I decided to lease the house for a few years. It would wait for me, so I thought back then. I called a couple who had been interested the year before. They jumped at the chance. That was easy, I thought.

Enter Joe. That is, of course, not his real name. And the story that follows is outright farfetched, seemingly too crazy to be real. Joe was a contractor in San Francisco, recommended to me by friends. He got the house ready for the next renters, painted the walls, fixed things here and there. He worked well and dependably – like a Swiss. Once in a while we talked, we got along well. Actually he was an artist, he said. In fact he had plans other than renovating houses. But the money was good.

Four days before I returned to Switzerland the prospective renters changed their minds. They didn't want to move after all. For a moment I was gripped by panic. How would I find renters in four days? Joe had a surprisingly simple suggestion: he was in the middle of a divorce and needed a place to stay, though he couldn't afford the rent. But he would pay half and work off the other half.

What a great idea! We made a list of jobs to be done, prioritized them and wrote up a contract for a year, after which it could be renewed every three months. Joe said he had it looked over by his lawyer. This is when I should've said, "good idea. I'll do that, too. Give me two days." But I didn't. I simply signed, relieved to have found such a great solution. "If you try any tricks on me, you won't have any friends left," I said jokingly. The first few months everything went well. Joe wrote enthusiastic emails from the "little house on the hill." Then the messages got sparser. I started worrying. He no longer sent reports or pictures, didn't respond to my emails, didn't pick up the phone. I handed the problem over to my then agent. She at least managed to get him to respond. But his messages grew extremely worrisome. They were confusing, accusatory and aggressive.

By the end of the agreed year the situation had gone completely off the rails. The next time I flew to San Francisco I intended to let Joe know I wouldn't renew the contract. But it turned out that in San Francisco you cannot terminate a rental contract after twelve months. Unless the rent is not paid. Since Joe sent his half in a timely fashion, I couldn't do anything. The fact that he didn't do the work he had agreed to was another issue.

"Why on earth did you sign that?" sighed my now-hired lawyer as he looked up from the contract. Good question. I didn't have an answer. Even the friends who had vouched for Joe only shrugged. "No one is in contact with him any longer," they said. "He even got kicked out of his local bar. He went nuts. Probably taking drugs."

I also learned that he wasn't in the middle of divorce but had been divorced for eighteen months when I met him. He simply refused to leave the house of his ex-wife. Like he did with me now. I could only hope he'd find a new victim soon.

The following years were a nightmare, though my then agent fielded most of the unpleasant phone tasks. I saw Joe only one more time. I demanded an inspection of the house after he had had the locks changed. Joe nailed a postcard to the front door with a skull on it. "Welcome Milena, ghost of Christmas spirit" it read.

I cried when I saw the blackened garden. The house, on the other hand, looked good. Joe had done the renovations that served him. He moved the toilet, built a new shelf in the bathroom – all at my cost. An optimistic friend said I should simply look into his eyes and he would see my good intentions and come to his senses. But when I did, I could see he felt I had done *him* an injustice.

Why didn't I sell the house after all that? When could I possibly live there? Years passed before he finally moved out, after which he sued *me* for half a million dollars. First, because I had forced him to live in subhuman conditions in an unlivable house. He claimed to have fallen down a rickety staircase that I had refused to fix, In reality the straightening of which was one of the top items on his list. After the fall, he said he'd become dependent on pain killers, unable to work, and "limited in his sexual functions." All my documentation, contracts and emails refuting his accusations, didn't help. The case dragged on. Six years it continued like that. The second part of my trip I would have to spend in San Francisco, going to appointments with lawyers, with insurance agents.

I haven't been able to live in my house in years, and still I love it. I always thought I'd move back there someday. To San Francisco. Into my house, my earlier life that I had left behind, not altogether willingly. With every year that passed, this objective slid farther into the background. What once was a concrete plan for the future turned into an almost unrealistic dream. But I kept talking about it. "One day I'll move back!"

But more and more it began to sound like "One day I'll win the lottery."

Susanne pops into my mind. The way she stands in the grass behind her house and for the first time I think: it doesn't have to be San Francisco. I could live anywhere. Wherever I have a home. The question simply is: what is home? Home is where the heart is. Home is where my sons are. Home is my desk. Maybe more than anything. The only thing that has never changed in my life. Whether I'm married, divorced, with small children or with adults. I am someone who writes. Does that mean I could live wherever there is a desk?

Does it have to be America? Why do I like it so much here? I can't explain. In San Francisco I paid taxes for eight years but could not work. I had to watch twice as they elected Bush, I sent my kids to private schools, I paid for my mammograms and other preventative medical treatments in cash. I picked up my kids from school in a car. I read in the paper that a neighbor's boy was shot. I have the same reservations as all my Swiss friends and yet... When I say I feel free here it sounds like a cliché. When I say I can breathe here it sounds silly. But that's how it is. I can't put any other words to it.

In Dallas, where I have to change planes, it is stormy. The plane sits on the runway for a long time, in the end we run more than two hours late. I sit between a budding psychologist, who confides that some of the behaviors he observed by the other passengers came up in psych lectures, and a retired army officer. Jodie, who with her short gray hair and military manner confirms my idea of a soldier, talks at me the whole time. She was stationed in New Mexico for a long time and knows her way around. Her suggestions sound like orders. "Take that road. Stop there! Order this!" Her secret tip is Madrid, stress on the first syllable. An old mining town along the Turquoise Trail, a favorite stop on motorcycle trips. "In the Mineshaft Tavern you have to order the green chili cheeseburger..." Suddenly Jodie's voice turns wistful. "I still own a small vacation home there," she says. "When I was in the army I needed it. I had to mix with the crazies, the freaks and the hippies on a regular basis. It was my balance to military life."

An air hostess brings a box with pretzels and nearly sings: "Good news! Since we've been stuck for two hours I can distribute the emergency rations!" I don't take one, and so later I get motion sick when the plane climbs over the mountains and abruptly drops down to Albuquerque. Someone takes my hand. It's not the young psychologist but the brisk Jodie. She doesn't let go of my hand even as we exit the plane, she pulls me along to the baggage claim and makes sure on the way that I heard what she told me. The airport of Albuquerque is decorated in turquoise and ocher and looks completely different from the airport in San Francisco or New Orleans or anywhere else. Un-American, I think and grin. The drive to Santa Fe takes over an hour. The road cuts through the mountain chain, the barren landscape is strangely familiar. I take a few wrong turns. It's dark when I arrive at Katchie's. I'm exhausted.

"It's the air," she says.

Thin Air: Katchie and Joshua

Air! That is my first impression. Finally breathing. The air is clear and thin and dry. In the Engadin, a Swiss mountain region with a similar altitude to here, they call it champagne air. After the oppressive humidity of Louisiana it's a great relief. That's my climate, I think. I get up early, Katchie makes me a smoothie, something healthy. The dog plays, the sky is expansive and endless. Two hammocks in the yard. She seems happy here. It shows.

Katchie was born in Switzerland but has lived for more than twenty years in the US and is one of the best known Western Yoga instructors. I got to know her in San Francisco. When I already knew we would return to Switzerland. A friend of mine, who was a news correspondent and who had more experience with moving around than I did, advised me not to make new friends, not to get to know any more locals. "It would be pure masochism," she said. But I lacked her discipline. I lived in San Francisco every day as if I would stay forever.

One day the phone rang. It was Katchie. In broad, somewhat old-fashioned Berndeutsch she explained that she had read my book Schlampenyoga [Slattern Yoga] and believed, nah, was sure that her classes were exactly what I needed. Back then she taught in the fashionable Mission District in her very own studio she later sold. Seventy, eighty students crowded into her classes – and she greeted them all with her brilliant smile – her trademark. Nobody has a bigger smile than Katchie. It filled the room and touched every single person. Just as her commentary during class reached everyone personally. I noticed that right away. She remembered names, test dates, vacation plans. Students brought their mothers who happened to be in town and who came to yoga in pantyhose. Those belonged in her class just as much as the rubber jointed future yoga teachers she trained.

She had just returned from Switzerland and had loaded up on Swiss chocolate. So she sat in lotus position in front of her harmonium and unabashedly chomped on her Lindt nut chocolate bar. Behavior that may appear normal in Switzerland, but that in the near fanatically health conscious Northern California yoga scene was about as radical as if she had snuck a cigarette before class. Some students looked suitably shocked. Katchie didn't flinch. "I need chocolate, it's in my genes," she happily declared. For that reason she had painted the ceiling of the yoga studio chocolate brown. When we lay on our backs and looked up at the ceiling we saw the sky as a gigantic chocolate bar. I liked that a lot. After class we went for coffee and forgot about time. Four hours later my phone rang. "Where are you? We have guests!" That was the beginning of a very special friendship which, due to my impending departure for Switzerland, acquired a certain urgency. After yoga class we always went for coffee and before we'd noticed, two hours had passed, parking tickets had accumulated, cell phones squeaked reproachfully. We became the kind of friends who don't have time for small talk. When we got together it was always about essentials.

A few years later she invited me to her wedding. I sat on the floor with crossed legs and cursed my elegant Swiss dress. I should've known that a Northern California wedding would be celebrated on the floor. I listened to the speeches, the wedding vows they had written themselves and thought of so often before. Joshua down deep is more Swiss than Katchie. Punctual, dependable and conscientious.

He doesn't say much but when he speaks, he means it. He doesn't make friends easily but he keeps them. Katchie, on the other hand, embodies everything I associate with America: a wild sense of freedom, an unshakable optimism, and an almost stubborn insistence on her own vision of happiness and her right to pursue it.

Katchie married a piece of Switzerland, I thought listening to the vows. A piece of the homeland. I thought back to her near magic story: after a great heartbreak, Katchie bought herself a pair of silver wedding bands and put them on two of the many arms of the dancing Hindu Goddess Shiva. Every day, she told me, she would pray in front of the statue: "Let me find my soul mate!" And when she flew back to Bern to be with her mother who had cancer, she said to her, "You can't die until I find him. You can't leave me alone."

One day a friend of Katchie's told her she met a guy in a cafe who would fit her. "Send him to my yoga class," she said. Then forgot about it. A few days later she noticed a tall man pass outside the studio whose long strawberry blond hair was tied in a braid. Katchie hesitated and followed him with her eyes: why is he passing instead of entering? she thought. Shortly thereafter he came in. It was Joshua, the man her friend had met in the cafe. After class they went to drink coffee. A few days later Katchie gave him a call as she was walking to her car, and when she looked up, there he was, ten yards away, phone to ear. When they had their first dinner date Katchie put all her cards on the table. "I am a strong woman," she said. "Many men have problems with that. And you?" As is his way, Joshua didn't immediately answer. Finally he explained that his roots were Mohawk, a matrilineal people led by women. Therefore he was used to strong women, after all his mother was one. But Katchie was not done. "And second, I'm not interested in a short-term relationship. I want a bond like wolves have. Wolves go their own way but they remain absolutely committed to each other."

It is important to understand that dates in America follow strangely archaic rules which, even after eight years in the country, remain foreign to me. The dating ritual is so rigidly structured that I often wondered how two people ever got together. For instance, a woman is absolutely forbidden to show interest or to call a man. If a first meeting should nonetheless happen, there is a whole checklist with how much money he makes at the top. What are his future prospects? Is he ready for a monogamous relationship? Does he want kids, if so, how many? On the men's list: is she uncomplicated, sexy, fun? So the men pretend to be more serious than they feel and the women more lighthearted. None admit to what they really want. If the two manage to convince each other of the opposite of what they really want, a second date is arranged. At the end of which comes a goodnight kiss. The chemistry has to be tested because by the third date sex is expected, finally – or, already?

However that may be, Katchie's behavior was utterly against the rules. But Joshua, twelve years her junior, remained calm. "Speaking of wolves – I spent part of my childhood on a reservation. My native name is Okwahoshatse which translates to "strong wolf." At the end of the evening Katchie dug the rings out of her pocket, where she had providently put them, and laid them on the table. Joshua slid the bigger one on his finger. It fit perfectly. He's still wearing it today. Shortly thereafter Katchie flew to Switzerland and told her mother about Joshua – after which she died.

Katchie and Joshua married a few years later, on the anniversary of mother's death.

"And they always told me I couldn't possibly find a husband in the Bay Area," she laughed. "They're all either gay or married."

For over a year now Katchie, Joshua and their dog Leelough have lived in Santa Fe. It was hard at the beginning. No one was waiting for her. At first she missed the crowded classes that had so oppressed her.

"What are you complaining about?" I ask, lazily swinging in the hammock and looking into the distance where the mountains frame the horizon like paper cutouts. I don't know why this landscape so deeply moves me. Why it seems so familiar. Katchie fits in here, even visually. She looks like a Native with her long dark hair and proud profile. More than her husband with all his native blood. I can see her galloping through an arroyo on her Palomino pony, wearing her fringed leather jacket. The thin air makes me breathless and tingly. Solicitously Katchie makes sure I drink lots of water. She mixes coconut oil with our morning smoothies to keep our skin supple. All at once I can see us, thirty years from now sitting here, two white haired women with parchment faces, who – while trying to heave themselves out of the hammock, burst out into uncontrollable giggles.

"Now you finally have time to write your book," I say "without the constant interruptions. Besides, you kept complaining about the strain of your weekly classes!" For me, this forced interruption in her schedule is a blessing. I can stay a whole week in the comfortable guest casita in Santa Fe. Katchie has lots of time for me. We drive here and there, she has prepared a detailed program, almost too much for me. But I love the countryside, I love the light. It feels so familiar. Only in New Mexico's history museum do I understand why: a whole gallery is dedicated to the books of Karl May. In the auditorium they show film clips of the old Winnetou films with Pierre Brice, dubbed in English. And even though I know these films were shot in the former Yugoslavia I still see it. It's exactly like that! It looks just right. The landscape touches an early romantic patterning...

... "Put this away!" my mother shouts. "You're way too young for it."

I didn't listen to her. I was in love. I don't know how old I was but I definitely didn't feel too young. I huddled under her desk where I could easily reach the bottom board of the bookshelf. That's where the

trade copies of her translations sat, among them an irreplaceable Swiss girl's treasure: the early novels of Federica de Cesco. *Der rote Seidenschal, Der Türkisvogel.*

Under the desk time stopped. Even though I had nothing in common with the young escapee who finds shelter with an Indian tribe and who, of course, falls in love with the son of the chief, I knew these books defined me. Had been written for me. This yearning for a place where the soul can be free... And now I'm here. Not exactly where the books took place, but a location that looks exactly how I used to imagine it.

And I'm by no means the only one. Santa Fe is a place of refuge, of retreat. Also a place where people relax. Retirement, I think. Madame Denise said it! Did she mean this place? This small town that had always been here for both, to retire and to find refuge. Many artists end up here. Painters seduced by the light that is particularly transparent here. Actors who filmed here and fell in love with the land. Rich divorced women in search of spiritual enlightenment, love, light. Many Northern European women, Swiss, Germans, all having grown up with Karl May and Federica de Cesco. Women like me?!

"I always wanted to live among the Natives," said Nathalie, a former fashion editor from Paris. "I had a teepee in my apartment in Paris." Now she manages a beautiful, very expensive shop in Santa Fe where she sells Indian jewelry and cowboy boots. She wears her long blond-gray hair in two braids down her back fastened by a headband and is festooned from head to toe with silver and turquoise. Katchie calls it the Santa Fe Style and warns me against it. "After a few years you can't stand to see it anymore!" Nathalie lets me have a pair of ankle-high cowboy boots with leopard print for half price. They're a bit small, but where there's a will... Her boyfriend Jim takes them from me, holds them in his hands gently like a pair of tiny animals. He thinks he can widen them a bit. Jim is not a Native but a wiry cowboy with a horseshoe mustache. In real life he's a photographer with a specialty. He has published three books, books of portrait studies – on cowboy boots.

At a dinner party a pretty, young, blond yoga instructor appears with a beautiful Native man. A Federica de Cesco dream couple. But then he begins to speak. At first he tells Espanola jokes. First off I think those are like Appenzeller jokes for Swiss or Ostfriesen jokes for Germans, gently poking fun at a specific part of the population. But the jokes this beautiful man tells have nothing good-natured about them. They are full of ugliness. Espanola is one of the poorest towns in New Mexico. The making and selling of drugs is about the only source of income. Its consumption the only diversion. "Do you know why the women in Espanola are no taller than five feet and have flat heads?" he asks me. I only stare at him. He's too drunk to notice I don't find his jokes amusing. "To have a place to put the beer while they..." He makes a rude gesture. "Exactly the right height, you see?" I nearly spit my soup at him. Complacently he goes on to an analysis of the Second World War: the Nazis were misunderstood, the Holocaust was blown out of proportion by the media. At some point I get up, excuse myself, "jet lag" I say and go to bed. As I pull the door shut behind me, I hear the sound of breaking glass. My girlish dreams smash on the tile floor. Such a beautiful Indian – and such an asshole! How is that possible? I would like to call

Federica de Cesco and ask her what she has to say. I would like to complain. In reality I'm the idiot. Reverse racism is still racism.

The next day we drive north to Ghost Ranch where Georgia O'Keeffe lived. "Well, well, well," she is supposed to have said when she got there. "Nobody told me it would be like that!"

Of Georgia O'Keeffe I only know the vaginal flower pictures that I, like most of my generation of latter day feminists, had tacked up above my bed as a student. I didn't know anything about her life or her work, and particularly I didn't know how much she hated this sexualization of her art. I leaf through a book about her life. The painter visited Santa Fe for the first time in 1917, on a trip to Texas. "Ever since then I've been on my way back..." Twelve years later she returned, in the midst of a work and marriage crisis – her husband, photographer Alfred Stieglitz, was also her agent. His needs defined her daily life between Manhattan and Lake George in Maine. He was constantly surrounded by family, students, artists and colleagues.

"I have to steal three weeks off to paint," Georgia complains. "And that is no way to paint." She found the landscape of Maine too lush and too green, the house too full of people, discussions, demands. She longed for solitude, the barrenness of the high desert, the wide sky of New Mexico. In the end Stieglitz himself encouraged her to leave. Not completely altruistically. Her last exhibition consisted mostly of older works. She hadn't been painting for a long time. And somehow he understood why that was. "Where Georgia is concerned, he wrote to a friend, Georgia is always a different person when she's free. Free from daily duties. And in an environment that matches (Land and Life) I knew that the

Southwest, exactly where she is right now, is THE right place for her. I saw the inevitability."

I let the book sink in. That could be me, I think. He could be writing about me. I know exactly what he means. That's how I feel.

"Ahh... would you like to buy the book?" asks the friendly volunteer in the gift shop.

"Yes, yeah, just a moment..." Randomly I turn pages in the book *Georgia O'Keeffe, A Life* by Roxana Robinson and I land in the year 1946, after the death of Alfred Stieglitz. "Her care for him was only surpassed by his need for emotional survival. Their relationship was of an immense tenderness, mutual support and respect, despite the tension between two artistic temperaments (...) and the inevitable strain of married life. Their connection was not completely conventional but utterly successful."

I swallowed emptily. That was exactly what my ex and I had wanted. A connection, not based on convention but on mutual support. We wanted to reinvent love, had grandiose ideas about freedom and spontaneity. The content of our relationship was supposed to mean more than its outer form. But every year we sank more deeply into conventions. In the end our marriage failed in the tritest way, like a petty bourgeois farce. The two-artist marriage doesn't work, I had resignedly decided. And now a barely understood idol from my idealistic youth proved the opposite. I nostalgically put Georgia and Alfred on the list of my dream couples.

"And?" the woman at the cash register was still waiting.

"Sorry." I blow my nose and pay for the book. Katchie, in the meantime, has checked out the seminar rooms. "We could do a workshop together here," she says. I agree immediately. I know absolutely beyond a doubt that I will return.

Welcome Home

The day before I'm due to leave, Katchie decides we have to check out Canyon Road with its incomparable density of galleries of local art. I don't know much about art but I know what I like. And what I don't: just about everything that is exhibited here, bronze bears, sunsets with horses, angels in night skies, hand-woven rugs that cost tens of thousands of dollars, Navajo pots behind glass. It's hot. On the road tourists throng, so too in the galleries. Then I see a sign: *Open House.*

"Come on, let's go look at a house for a change," I say. It's a kind of hobby of mine. I always keep an eye out for the real estate signs, check their offerings as though I were seriously interested. In my mind I furnish the loft in Hamburg, the attic apartment in Paris, the converted mill in the country. I also often dream of apartments and houses, see every detail, every nook and cranny, very clearly. When I wake up I could draw them. The rooms I've dreamt about are as familiar as if I'd lived in them.

We follow the sign into the back courtyard of a gallery and through an open door in the wall that leads onto a tiny patio. A double door, then a living room. I sink onto the window seat, look at the tiny patio and think: Ah, it's lovely to be home after such a long trip. Excuse me? Be home? I get up, the house is full of people, it's tiny. A square room, divided by curtains. A bedroom, a kitchen, a tiny bathroom. The living room with the window seat, a fireplace. Thick, irregular, whitewashed mud walls, white beams on the ceiling. At the entrance hang dried chili pepper strings. It's traditional but not rustic. I give it a quick look, everything's familiar, like home. So much so that the other visitors soon get on my nerves. Why are they tramping around my house?! This is my house!

I've had this feeling twice before, once in San Francisco, once in Aarau. I was happy in both places. Was? I am happy in Aarau. I've lived in the apartment for two years, a place fate arranged for me when I was looking for a home after my hasty departure from our dream house. The first weeks I lived in a studio I had rented next to my writing workshop. During my marriage one certainty grew: I need my alone time. It's part of me. When I'm alone I regenerate, I become myself. Now that I'm really alone, I'm not so sure any longer. Maybe I simply needed to recover from my marriage.

After the separation I found the apartment in Aarau. It is my refuge. Every time I come home I'm content. When I was doing so badly that I couldn't go outside the front door and was lying on the sofa in the bay window crying for weeks, all I had to do was open the window to hear life in the old town alleys and realize: it's all here. Life goes on. Right outside my house. When I'm ready I go down the stairs and I'm right in the midst of it.

Here in Santa Fe it's similar. The little house sits hidden and quiet only ten steps from the busiest street of the city. The uneven thick walls keep the noise out, the old trees bow protectively over the seating area. But the silence, the seclusion can be abandoned any time – right away you're smack dab in the middle of pulsating life.

On the table lies a brochure advertising the house. "An ideal home for a writer," it says. I know, I think, I know! The real estate agent comes up to me, hands me a card. "Hello, Herr Nuescheler," I say and pronounce his name in Swiss. He's taken aback. "Most people call me Mister Natschler," he says.

"Well, yes, I'm from Switzerland..."

"Me, too!" he shouts. Or at least his grandfather who had emigrated from Grindelwald was. We talk a bit about the house. Then I turn to Katchie, who's still waiting, and say "I have to have a drink. I've got to sit down. My knees are shaking."

On the street a tall man with mirrored sunglasses comes up to us. "So, girls, is the Casita pretty enough for you?"

"Are you the owner?" Katchie asks.

That he is. His name is Frederic. Katchie asks him the most important questions right off: what's the parking situation, is the roof in good shape? I'm not really listening. We go to the Teahouse where Natalie Goldberg famously wrote *Writing Down the Bones.* I ignore the four-page tea menu and order a double espresso despite the fact I'm already jittery. I don't know what's happening to me. I think I'm in love. "Katchie," I say "I think I've got to buy this house."

I don't have any money. I have a house in San Francisco with a curse on it, an absurd and endless legal battle. The last thing I would've imagined was buying yet another house. Especially not in a place where I have no connections other than a happy couple that lives here. Especially not on a street where I get bombarded with bad art. But there's this really strong feeling: this is my home. So we go back. In the meantime everyone has left. The real estate agent and Frederic sit on garden chairs and drink Tequila with grapefruit juice. They offer us drinks. "No, thank you," I say "I feel drunk already."

I look everything over once more. The house is really tiny, about five hundred square feet, but cleverly set up, every corner functional. I could move in immediately. I wouldn't change anything. Again I land on the window seat.

"This is my favorite spot, too," says Frederic. I talk to him like an old friend. I feel as though, like with his house, we'd been acquainted for a long time. Suddenly I have a vision: I see a tiny Christmas tree next to the fireplace, my two sons sprawled on the sofa. I'm imagining Christmas here. What an absurd thought. Christmas holds the most painful wound from the separation. Christmas weighs on me the whole year. And suddenly there's an alternative. At least in my imagination. As unrealistic it is, it's comforting. I put my hand on my heart to keep the image safe.

Today's Sunday, tomorrow Monday, Memorial Day, a holiday. Monday night I depart; I fly back to New York and then Switzerland for the mis-scheduled performance. The first part of my trip is finished. That evening I talk to Katchie and Joshua. I'm excited as it feels as though I were indeed in love.

"Good thing Frederic is gay," I say "or I'd fall for him too."
"Gay?" Katchie asks. "What makes you say that?"

"Isn't it obvious?" Though I was never very good at recognizing such a thing. Eight years in San Francisco didn't sharpen my 'gay-dar.' Basically a person's sexual orientation only interests me if I'm interested in him. But I didn't want to go there. I blush.

"I don't really want to remain alone forever," I told Frederic. "I wouldn't want to live in a house in which only I could fit. I wouldn't want to cement my singleness." I would never have said such a thing to a straight man. How embarrassing.

Frederic only laughed and said that he had certainly had "partners" in the last seven years but only a special person could fit in this house. Gays say "partner" don't they?

"You've been caught," Joshua pinpoints, but he means something different. "You have the Adobe fever!" It catches most people when they first get here. They are attracted by the expanse, the space, and the relatively cheap real estate prices. They can afford something bigger here, and there is space. The typical Santa Fe house is a one-story sprawling adobe structure with a lot of land and a broad view, all the way to the blue mountains at the horizon. I don't particularly like adobe architecture, I find it kitsch. The house doesn't have a view. But it has thick walls that close around me protectively. It is tiny. It is perfect. It is my house.

Katchie calls her real estate agent Lisa who promises to come see the house the following day despite the holiday. "The price is right," she says. "I'd snatch it up. How are you going to do it?"

"Well, I'll have to take out a loan," I say. "I'll call my bank in Switzerland. It isn't a holiday there today."

I already know what my banker, Mr. Perez, will say. He'll try to talk me out of it. I think up the arguments to convince him. I have a personal, almost familial, connection to my bank, even if that sounds ridiculous. My grandfather, a lonely, gloomy man I barely knew, had fallen in love for a second time late in life. His wife whom we called Tante Klaerli came from Lenzburg, where this small bank with only a handful of branches is situated. And my grandfather put all his money there. Out of love.

My grandfather died when I was nine and left me quite a bit of money – at least that was how it appeared to me. When I turned twenty-one and could legally access the money I wasn't really a grown-up yet. The train ride from Zurich to Lenzburg seemed endless at the time, and if anyone had told me I would end up living near there, I would've laughed.

First I opened an account. A solemn moment. Then I received the money and traveled to Paris where I managed, in a very short time, to spend it all. I have no idea how that happened. All I remember is having lots of visitors. And that we liked ordering colorful cocktails in flower vases decorated with umbrellas and plastic giraffes. Maybe it has something to do with those drinks that I remember so few details. In retrospect, though, it was not wasted time because that's when I started writing. Seriously writing.

I didn't dare call it that back then. Having grown up in a literary household, I hadn't met a single female writer. In my childhood there were only wives of writers, and writers like my father, serious men with at least university degrees, who smoked pipes and discussed how they would change the world. I didn't want that. I wanted to tell stories. I just didn't know how to do it. From the age of eight I carried note books where I scribbled diary type sentences and sometimes a bad poem. The leap into fiction appeared to me as presumptuous and dangerous as the leap from our roof into the yard. An adventure of which my first friend tried to persuade me. He was a bit older than I was, already in Kindergarten and, unlike me, he was allowed to watch TV. And not just children's programs but series where real shooting happened, for instance *Daktari*. He often talked about *Daktari* and after I begged him for a long time he relented to play *Daktari* with me. It went like this: we stood under the porch, armed with long wooden sticks, and tried to knock off the snow while shouting "Daktari, Daktari!" And when the snow fell from the roof we ran away. It would've been better to jump from the porch roof into the snow piles but my mother caught us and so it stayed with the sticks. Soon afterwards he moved away. As a parting gift he gave me a cardboard box and a shell. He promised to cut a hole in the bottom of the car to let himself fall out and return to me. We were going to get married. I never heard from him again. Years later I saw *Daktari* on TV. The series takes place in Africa. There is a cross-eyed lion and a monkey, but absolutely no trace of snow.

After finishing my apprenticeship in an arts bookstore, I went to Paris under the pretext of taking French classes. I connected with a group of budding filmmakers who met weekly to discuss their life dreams and plans while smoking lots of cigarettes. In that environment, I dared say it out loud for the first time. When asked what I did I answered boldly, "I'm a writer."

Maybe because no one knew me. Maybe because I was speaking a foreign language. In any case, no one broke out in wild laughter. No one yelled, "Who, you? You got to be joking!" No, the question that mainly followed was, "And, you got published yet?"

"No," I answered truthfully. "Non." But that wasn't serious; the filmmakers had the same problem. We were young. We stood, so to speak, on the starting blocks. We discussed our projects and I'll never know if the others exaggerated as fearlessly as I did. I spoke of short stories and the beginnings of a novel, while in reality all I had were observations from my daily life scribbled in a Chinese notebook, black with red corners. Maybe the film projects of my new friends were as much a pipedream as my novel. But I almost got used to my identity as writer whose only missing piece was the actual writing. But fate or happenstance had a young German join our group, who of course wanted to read something of mine. Because I write in German, my French friends never asked.

I had talked myself into a corner. Out of which I now had to write myself. "Sure, no problem," I said and went home to write three very short stories, strongly reminiscent of my then favorite authors, before the next meeting. The German was not impressed. "Interesting," was all he said. But it was a beginning.

Next I claimed to be writing a novel. We sat on the floor in the home of a young musician and I looked around the room, stole a line from a poster here and a sentence from a conversation there. "Ah, yes, my novel is called *Late at Night* and deals with a, ahem, musician, no a photographer named Biba who..."

Later I sat on the toilet and wrote in my Chinese notebook, "*Late at Night*, A Novel."

That's how it started. That's how I began to invent. To blur the boundaries between the various realities. The first step into the void was the easiest. The snow was so high that I could step directly from our porch roof into the soft cold white. Everything was already there. Apes and lions, staves and snow. Lies, fantasies, dreams and images – my head was full of them. All I had to do was write them down.

That was how three months and my inheritance passed. And that was why, when the money began to run out, I wrote a letter. To my bank. That was before ebanking and ATM machines. I wrote long letters on the manual typewriter from which my first novel came into being. I explained my situation in flowery, and I hoped, convincing language. For my evolution as a writer it was vital that I remain in Paris. But I was lacking some funds to bridge what I was sure to be only a short period of time until I had found a publisher.

It took more than six years until my first novel came out. Six years during which I would leave Paris and take various day jobs. But I did end up getting the money – an investment in my future.

Years later when I came into that very bank, which still looked the same, with the big check from a real publisher, the clerk remembered my letter from long ago. To be honest, he confessed, he hadn't totally believed in my success. He had worried about me. But now it was all good.

My bank shares in my life. I trust it. So I will bow to the verdict of Mr. Perez. In the meantime I allow myself daydreams that flit through my mind like short films. I see myself planting a lavender bush with a straw hat on my head. I see myself galloping on a small horse behind Katchie. The hat falls off. I see myself sit on Frederic's red garden chair reading, forgetting the time. All at once something begins to stir inside me which I haven't felt for a long time and for good reasons. It's my life, I suddenly feel. It's becoming my own life. Soon I'll be able to ask: what do I want? How do I want to live?

I don't allow myself these questions yet. Not quite. But I feel that one day I'll get there. One day, soon. Lisa drives me to her office to fill out a purchase agreement. Then I sit in the Teahouse again. I wait for Joshua. He wanted to look at the house again. I call a friend who knows New Mexico well. She is instantly excited. "You belong there," she says. "I can easily imagine you there." Joshua doesn't show up so I call Frederic. "Joshua's already come and gone," he says. "Do you want to come by another time?" "No," I say. "It's not necessary. I'll make an offer in the next couple of days."

"Now I have weak knees," he says.

Alone with Bette and Nurse Gloria

When I get back to New York everything has changed. Gabriele has a new roommate: Miss Pickles, a nine week old fox terrier that needs to be walked every few hours. Through the university where Gabriele works she makes arrangements for a room in a fancy hotel on the Upper West Side, at a discount rate reserved for foreign lecturers. I feel like Woody Allen. And like an impostor. In the elevator I sometimes catch myself looking into the mirror and wonder if I could pass as a lecturer. It also reminds me of a taxi driver who once picked me up at the Burghoelzli, the psychiatric university hospital in Zurich. It was pouring rain. "Did you visit someone?" he asked. I shook my head. "Then you're a doctor?" – "That either." Now there's only one possibility. The driver looked into the rearview mirror, inspected me closely. I held his gaze. Maybe I even smiled. "Don't worry," he said, "you could easily pass as a doctor."

When I lived in Zurich, near the Burghoelzli, I always held my breath passing by the entrance. "There but for the grace of God go I..." Not infrequently was I tempted, instead of continuing on to the tram station, to push the door of the clinic open and tell the receptionist: "I'm ready. May I come in?"

A thin line separates me from insanity, the hint of a discrepancy, a paper-thin wall through which I could step at any point.

I could also pass as a doctor. Or a guest lecturer.

I spend the following days on the phone and computer, trying to collect data and documents, staying awake late into the night to catch Mr. Perez in Switzerland, and getting up early in the morning to speak to Lisa and Pete in Santa Fe.

65

Mr. Perez, against all expectations, is delighted with the house and considers it a wonderful idea, a good investment. "We'll make this possible! But you won't get a loan in Switzerland, he says. Not for an investment in America. Not when the only collateral is another house in America. Not in this climate." I call Lisa who expected a scenario like this. She says it could get tricky and gives me Pete's address. "If anyone can make it possible, he can." Pete is a mortgage broker in Santa Fe and a writer manqué. Thirty-five years ago he worked in a psychiatric clinic and wrote a novel during the long hours of night-watch. He can't remember what he wrote but he would love to show it to me. A few days later he mails me the manuscript that had sat in a drawer for thirty-five years. He not only mailed it to me but also three friends, one of whom is a literature professor. That one promises to read it and, possibly, to recommend a publisher. "Without you," says Pete, "without our conversation I would never have dared." Only he can't get me a loan either. I no longer have a valid visa.

Mr. Perez says the only realistic possibility is to ask my mother or brother for money. I don't want to do that. Combining money and friendship is not a good idea. Money and family, even less so. Money and family is a minefield. Lessons I have learned slowly and painfully. Lessons I cannot simply ignore.

I give up. I tell Frederic, "I'm sorry, I have to withdraw my offer." He's been sending me emails several times a day, with links to all possible locales and sights in Santa Fe. I will miss those messages. But he doesn't stop writing, sending me little anecdotes and tips. He won't let me forget the city. And the house even less.

Now I intend to enjoy the final two days in New York. In my hotel room the suitcases are bursting. I have already bought too much and keep buying more: floor-length tee shirt dresses, flat shoes, gifts, cosmetics, vitamins you can't buy in

Switzerland – as if I weren't returning to US soil two weeks later. My oversize purse, I only just notice, has rubbed all my clothes and sweaters on one side, leaving thin and fuzzy patches. I have to buy a new purse. No, clothes. The trip is already more expensive than planned, even without buying a house. And I haven't even started writing about this trip in order to make some of the money back. I meet with Little Kate, the oldest daughter of Paul and Daphne, who works as a nanny a few streets away. Little Kate is no longer little but we still call her that. Half a year ago Little Kate stood at the airport in New York where she had been visiting friends and was on the way home to her parents. She had checked her baggage in and stood at the gate. She pulled her cell phone out of her pocket to turn it off.

"But I couldn't," she said, still surprised at the certainty that arose from nowhere. "I couldn't turn off the phone, I couldn't get on the plane, I couldn't leave the city."

At this point in her narrative I imagine Little Kate in a phone booth laboriously dialing a number; that would satisfy the dramatics of the moment better. But there are no more phone booths and no more dial phones, and the New York airport probably wasn't swathed in fog as the young woman called home and announced she wouldn't return.

"I just knew," she says and in her voice the relief is still audible. I know what she means. Hardly anything is more difficult to handle than uncertainty. What am I going to do with my life? Where am I going? What would be right? Instead, we calm ourselves with the idea that life could be lived along straight paths and planned in five year increments. Life, however, resists and shakes off plans like bothersome flies. I think of the little house in Santa Fe. I felt the same certainty as Little Kate. But I could not carry through. All the more I find comfort in her story. The no longer Little Kate had to conjure up a job and an apartment. Which is not easy to do in New York and even less so in Manhattan. But as always when you suddenly know the next step, the one after that shows up too. You put one foot in front of the other and step through open doors. Kate found a job as nanny, badly paid but with food and lodging. The mother was Swiss. "Don't worry about my tone," she warned Kate, "I'm not rude, I'm Swiss!"

"That's OK," Little Kate said. "I grew up among Swiss people." That included me as well. I'm touched as I remember the small role I played as her neighbor and friend. I, too, had to often explain myself in San Francisco. "I'm not angry, I'm Swiss," an explanation that is accepted everywhere. Maybe I'm too old to start over. Maybe you have to be young, like Little Kate, and unattached to be able to follow that voice. Or you have to drag the others along. As we did back when the four of us moved to San Francisco. I already experienced a new life. I already had a chance to start over. I gave it up, in exchange for security.

On my cell I have a series of pictures of the house in Santa Fe. Over and over I look through them and sigh like a love-sick teenager. What is it this house promises? What wishes would it fulfill for me? I think again of Georgia O'Keeffe. The first time she saw what would be her house in Abiqui it was in ruin. Not much more than a wall with a door. But "that wall with a door in it was something I had to have."

I only want a place where I can be myself. With people who take me as I am. That's all. Is that so hard? Couldn't that be in Aarau or Zurich?

The last evening I spend by myself. I manage to score a ticket for a one woman play starring Bette Midler. A monologue based on the autobiography of Sue Menkes, the legendary Hollywood agent. The ticket costs more than a night at my hotel. I don't care. It's my last night. Half of my trip is over. Tomorrow I fly back to Switzerland, the day after I myself will be on stage again. I can hardly remember the woman I was at the beginning of my trip, the woman who laughed in the subway after nobody wanted to dance with her. I barely remember the pouring rain. It's hot and muggy in New York and icy cold inside every building.

I drive to Broadway, sit in the next best restaurant. It looks like a tourist trap, a chow hall, I don't care. The place is packed, I sit at the bar. I order fried calamari, an appetizer that comes on a platter big enough to feed a whole family. On the TV screen relentless rain falls, somewhere a hurricane threatens. Outside it's day and still nearly ninety degrees. I sit between two couples and talk to the waiter. On my left the young man in old-fashioned clothes explains the difference between psychoanalysis and psychotherapy to a somewhat older woman. For a while I listen with interest, my eyes glued to the TV screen so he won't notice. On my other side the man excuses himself and the woman turns to me: "Don't you think he should at least order me another drink?" She points out her empty glass. "He could at least act as if the evening was going well."

I am no expert in relationships I want to say, but then I shrug. Why not? I have learned a thing or two along the road. "How long have you known each other?" I ask.

"Oh, honey, it's our first date!" she spreads her fingers as though showing off her fancy manicure. She is dressed to the nines, made up, hair done. Hours, I think. Hours she must have spent getting ready. She gives the bartender a meaningful look, he refills her glass.

"Oh!" Now I don't know what to say. "I don't know the rules," I apologize, "I'm not from here." In Switzerland, I want to say, where I come from, a woman can call a man without seeming desperate. She can even invite him home to dinner without signaling romantic intention or expectation. But if I'm honest, I don't know if that is still true. It's been twenty years since I did something like that.

The final years of my marriage I lived under a glass bubble. That was the way it was supposed to be, I had to dissolve the existing relationship without being sidetracked by a new love. Falling in love with someone new is the easiest way out of a relationship. I knew that already – from experience. I am absolutely no saint. But this time it wouldn't work. I gripped my marriage as hard as a bulldog on a slipper. When I finally let go I experienced the emptiness around me as soothing. A relief. Only my vanity was hurt. Why am I alone? Why is nobody willing to catch me? Until now there was always someone. From the age of fourteen there was always at least one man. I loved each and every one of them. Each of them molded my life. Changed it. Or you could say: with every one I turned my life on its head. Whether he wanted that or not. "I've never known a woman who so completely dissolves in love," one of them said once. That's my name, Milena. It literally means "the much loved". Or, the loving one. Sometimes it seems ironic, but deep inside, it fits. Only when I'm in love, when I am loved, do I forget that I'm a mistake, that I shouldn't actually exist. That I am not enough.

Of course in this difficult phase, too, I wish someone would come and rescue me. Or at least distract me. Someone for whom I could turn my life upside down again. Someone for whom I could abandon work. Only in the arms of a man can I forget the time, while away the days, miss appointments and deadlines. Love conquers all. Doesn't it?

But then something strange happened: where I used to have the feeling that the world was jam packed with gorgeous men and my biggest challenge was to choose the right one, suddenly there was nothing. No one. A man-less desert. It was as if only women and children passed before my eyes. Through my daily life. Even the streets seemed swept clean, the Internet even more so, the phone stayed silent. Not even on TV did I see men I liked. That had always been my married American friends' solution: instead of falling in love with a flesh and blood man they developed TV crushes and spent hours, if not nights, in the company of Dr. Shepherd or Marshal Raylan Givens. A surprisingly satisfactory and pragmatic solution. Unfortunately even with my TV crushes I tend to conform to my favorite of the moment. And the worst is: I don't even notice. "Hey, why are you swearing so much?" a friend asks. "From my crush on Al Swearengen from Deadwood," I realize.

The woman who sits next to me at the bar of Big Daddy's Diner looks at her watch. Her date hasn't returned. "He bailed," she says impassively, puts twenty dollars on the counter and leaves.

In the theater I sit next to an elderly woman with fantastic golden hair the likes of which I've only seen on TV. We begin talking and it turns out she's an author too. She has written a book about her Armenian mother that is just coming out and before the curtains rise I have practically promised to find her a German publisher.

The performance starts and I forget everything else. That doesn't happen very often. Most of the time my mind drifts. But this time I'm completely awake, I am present. I feel Bette Midler, or rather Sue Menken, speaks directly to me. About the meaning of fame and success, the survival chances of friendships in the public eye. I nod, I laugh, I lose myself in the play. In one scene she tells how she tried to convince Ali McGraw, who had retired, to do one final big role. But when she saw her in the doorway, a baby on her hip, glowing with happiness – "I knew I had no chance. I didn't even get out of the car. With true happiness Hollywood cannot compete." I feel a tiny stab. Not because I wonder if individual happiness excludes the professional or the other way around, but because the scene takes place in Santa Fe. Santa Fe is a tiny wound that burns. A paper cut. As if I had been allowed a glimpse of a variant of my life, a possibility. But only a glimpse. Then the curtain falls.

After the final applause the audience presses for the exits. I recognize a face in the crowd: that's Nurse Gloria. From the series *Nurse Jackie*! I fold my hands near my heart, bow and shout, "We love you in Switzerland!" The actress smiles noncommittally.

This evening I'm happy. I need nothing. I miss nothing. It is enough. I hardly remember the woman who arrived here five weeks ago: exhausted, insecure and under enormous pressure to finally be happy. I walk back through streets that are not mine. It's still hot. The first part of my trip has reached its end.

PART TWO:

HAPPINESS HAS FOUR WALLS

Google Happiness

When I get back to Switzerland Frederic sends me a small video he had taken with his cell phone. He speaks into the camera, his voice a bit nervous: "it's been a week since I got to know you," he says, "Yes, you – and it was wonderful."

I show the clip to my girlfriends, I am confused, what does it mean? What does this man want? "He's flirting with you," they say. "Why gay, what made you think that? He's not gay!"

No? I allow myself a tiny inner smile, a softening. Really, he's flirting with me? So maybe it's not about the house after all? Maybe I didn't get a loan because really I was supposed to meet this man? I visit girlfriends, I let myself get caught up in the story, I talk about the house, the man, I collect opinions left and right but notice that I only want to hear one thing: "He's not gay, he likes you!"

Why? Because it's what I've been wanting: to meet a man who feels familiar, like an old friend. A man with whom I feel comfortable enough not to worry about what I say or what I look like. A man who doesn't scare me.

He sends one more film clip in which he leafs through his diary. In a lower corner he's drawn me with my curls and a speech bubble: "I'm going to make an offer." And underneath he wrote: "I allow myself to hope."

I allow myself to hope? I allow myself to hope! He sends one clip after another and I begin to think of him in a different way. It's been a long time since I felt even such a small innocent tingle. About a year after our separation, it had happened for the first time that a man who appeared in my field of vision made me pause. I saw him from afar on the other side of the street, a serious face, deep set eyes. "Hmmm…" This awareness, this tiny interest had been absent for so long, I almost didn't recognize it. I had to cross the street to look at his face on the poster close up. It was John Cage. Dead for twenty years. But still, a beginning."Your next goal is one who's still alive," said a friend who'd been watching me with an indulgent smile.

No. The next goal is myself. "The next love story you'll have with yourself" – I don't remember who told me that. But it was right. So I accept at first with gnashing teeth, then with relief, that for now no man shall cross my field of vision. For my own protection.

But Frederic is not real. He can't get too close, he can't get dangerous. Almost daily he sends me messages and video clips; he tells me something from his own life and thus forces his way into mine. Over and over he tells me about the new open house events, shows me the crowds rolling through "my" rooms. The tiny house. My house. Where I saw myself celebrating Christmas with my sons. My unlived life.

One evening I sit on the sofa with my laptop on my knees and a glass of wine in hand. The performance went well. In three days I will fly back to San Francisco, meet my lawyer, then continue my trip. My next stop is Stephensville, Montana, where my cousins live on a horse ranch in a breathtakingly beautiful landscape. Marina and her husband Chris are definitely on my list of happy couples. Also, she has deep connections in the nearby reservations; maybe she could take me to a Sundance Ceremony. But Marina writes to say that my dates don't work very well for her. Her family runs a summer camp for teens, with horseback riding, painting, dancing. I could participate, she offers. Or maybe lead a creative writing group? I will think about it. But maybe instead I should return to Santa Fe? To discover what it was that I can't let go of -- the town, the house, or the man. It's rather late when I begin to Google Frederic. I click on images. The first one is a concert poster of an English musician with the same name, "In concert with Stephen Porter," it says underneath. Stephan Portner is the name of my brother. It's a sign! Maybe I've had one glass too many. But at this moment it seems very clear: I have to ask my brother if he would lend me the money.

He will. I write Frederic immediately. "I've decided to return to Santa Fe next week. Will you be there?"

In his return video clip he laughs nervously, "And – will you sleep in *your* house?"

Lake Milena: A Dream

I sit in the doorway of "my" house in Santa Fe. Yes, it's my house. That is very clear in the dream, as is the fact that I haven't just recently moved there. It's exactly how I remember it. Except instead of a small patio, there is a lake. I sit on the doorstep and dangle my feet in the water. The horizon is wide and I cannot see the other shore. A bird settles on the water near me. The sun goes down, it gets cool. I pull my feet out of the water and wrap my arms around my legs. Soon I'll get up and go inside. Someone is in the house, a man, I can't see him, I don't know who he is, only that he is there. I turn to him and say: "yes, I could live like that."

On the Road Again

The second half of my trip begins in San Francisco. The lawyer brings bad news: Joe's lawsuit is moving forward. I will have to appear in court. There is no date yet. Contrary to the Swiss system, in America the burden of proof is with the accused. So I will have to prove it's not my fault that Joe fell down the stairs. If that even happened. I gather emails, contracts, correspondence. My lawyer passes them on to the insurance. Nothing in me understands what's happening. No one I tell the story to can understand. Sometimes I fear not even my lawyer understands. Worst Case Scenario: I lose the house. If Joe wins, I'll have to sell the house to pay him off.

What I hear most often during this time: "I told you, you should have sold the house! This is what you get!" Second most: "why don't you sue *him* if it's that easy?" I admit I got close. But my lawyer remained decent. "I don't advise it. Guys like those have nothing. And if there is anything it'll all be eaten up by lawyers' fees." The next step is to convince my insurance to take the case. The lawyer coaches me on the phone. "Don't talk about the renovation work he was supposed to do for you, or the case comes back to me and then it will cost you." He charges three hundred dollars an hour but lets me pay him in Sprüngli chocolates. For years I didn't receive a bill from him. Sometimes I think he feels sorry for me. That doesn't exactly make me feel good. But his strategy works, the insurance takes the case, at the moment there's nothing left for me to do. I want to get out, I want to continue my trip, I feel something big is going to happen. Something that will change my life.

Early in the morning I leave the City swathed in the usual thick summer fog behind me. I drive across the Bay Bridge, direction south, not along the beautiful coast highway but on the straight Interstate 5. My navigation system says I should arrive to my friend Lil's house in the desert in eight hours. Immediately my competitive mind starts: all I have to do is trick the GPS – ha, ha! I was quicker than you thought! I neither notice the landscape nor do I stop anywhere to look around. Impatiently I fiddle with the radio knob. When I find music I like and begin to listen until I understand the words, invariably it turns out to be some Christian station. I don't even have an Ipod. Who goes on a trip like this without any preparation?

Suddenly I realize I've driven on this road before. I wanted to write a book about a road trip before, a novel that time, called *Not Quite Vegas*. I drove from San Francisco to Las Vegas alone in my silver battleship, a Cadillac from the eighties, for research purposes. My American friends laughed about that car. They called it the pimpmobile. But I believe every European who moves to America falls prey to the temptation to drive such a battle wagon. All those films haven't passed us by without leaving traces. The pictures that shaped us are stronger than our consciences, consideration of the environment, or the cost of fuel. The pimpmobile gave up the ghost near Newman, California. I managed to make it to the hard shoulder. Fortunately a friend had given me her insurance card. There was a phone number for a towing service. So my Caddie and I were saved on the road, towed to Newman where a mechanic thought he could patch it together so I could make it home. "But you won't get to Las Vegas, Miss!"

"Do you have a gun with you?" said another. "A woman shouldn't drive through the desert without a gun."

"And water – you don't have any water?"

There I was again, badly prepared for my trip. One of the older men hanging out at the garage offered to take me out. There was a restaurant in town called Le Paris where for $5.95

you could eat all you want. Jim told me a bit about his hometown. "We are the meth capital of California," he said proudly. When he stressed that his last name Schwartz was German, not Jewish, just so I wouldn't get any wrong ideas, I said goodbye. My car was ready. I returned to San Francisco. I ate a hamburger on the road, I remember, because I normally never do. My whole trip lasted less than twenty-four hours.

This makes me laugh. I should've known I'm not built for road trips. I want to get there. Not be on the road. For a moment I consider stopping in Newman to see if Le Paris still exists. But already the exit is past. It always happens like this: the impulse to stop and look is pushed aside by the urge to get there, to arrive. The road is not the goal. Not for me. Thank God, I think. I'm so glad I didn't go through with my initial plan of a three month road trip. After just two days behind the wheel my shoulders are frozen in place.

I arrive at Lil's near evening. Tomorrow is her birthday and the house is full of women. We speak about relationships and I talk about my marriage. I tell them that at the end I was so insecure I couldn't even cross a public square without tensing up. My ex felt my uncertainty, felt how I stiffened and stopped, "When you get like that I don't want to go anywhere with you." We would turn around and drive home without speaking. I cried, despairing, why was I like that? Why couldn't I do anything right anymore? But also: Why doesn't he love me the way I am? Sometimes shy, sometimes self confident? Because the same woman who couldn't cross a square "correctly" on his arm, could get on a stage the next day and entertain an audience.

Lil frowns. "I've never seen you this dependent, " she says. And, "You sound as though you haven't gotten over the whole thing yet!" I suppose she's right about that – but it's not the man I can't forget, it's the woman I became by his side. The woman I never want to be again. But somewhere inside she's still there, the readiness to bend in this or that direction. Lil doesn't know everything because I haven't told her everything. I've never told anyone because I was ashamed about the misery of my marriage. I was ashamed that I had let it go that far.

"Try this," Lil says, "Just don't talk of the past any longer. Don't let it influence the present."

That reminds me of something I read in one of Pam Houston's autobiographical essays, "I am adult enough to recognize the two big tokens I received in the psyche lottery: I cannot remember really bad things and I have never quite grasped the concept of shame."

Somewhere I wrote the sentence down. It made perfect sense. Despite, or maybe because of, the fact I didn't draw those two tickets, I recognize their importance. Maybe I can fake it till I make it!

It's worth a try. The ability to be happy can be trained like a muscle. I read that somewhere too.

I continue on, stay overnight somewhere in Arizona. "Standin' on the Corner Park in Winslow Arizona..." Again I have that feeling that hits me so often in America: I know this place. I've been here before. If you've watched enough movies you've been everywhere. The *Posada* in Winslow is the most beautiful of the Harvey Hotels, a masterpiece by the architect Mary Colter. Fred Harvey was the man who tamed the Wild West by introducing tablecloths, porcelain, crystal glasses and silverware in the railroad dining cars to Santa Fe as well as in the rest stops en route. His employees were called the Harvey Girls, wore special uniforms and had excellent manners. It was an honor to be a Harvey Girl. Judy Garland played one in a movie in 1946. The hotel closed down in 1957 but reopened forty years later, lovingly and faithfully renovated. And still, I'm disappointed; the hotel is huge and crowded. Well, after all, it's mentioned in every guide book. Buses line up outside, tourists crowd the lobby. Most of them don't stay the night; they visit the place like a museum, a gift store. Everywhere there are souvenirs for sale, even at the bar.

In the dining room I'm suddenly uncomfortable. I feel as though I'm the only one traveling alone. I never minded it before. But now I feel as though I'm disturbing the flow, as if I'm unsettling the staff. "Should we seat someone with you?" The smallest table is for four. I think of the nice conversations on the train to New Orleans. But tonight I don't feel up for it.

"No, that's OK."

"Hm."

After dinner I return to the parking lot to get my computer cable from the trunk. When I go to open it I can't find my car keys. Since this happens all the time I know what to do. I turn my purse over onto the still hot tarmac. Nothing. I peak inside the car. Did I leave it in the ignition? Nothing there. I didn't open my purse in my room. I start walking – but I don't return to the hotel, instead I walk along the train tracks back to town. It's still hot and almost light. The full moon hangs in the sky looking like a second sun.

For one moment I'm almost relieved. I lost my car key; that means I cannot continue. That means I cannot buy the house. I don't have to change my life. I won't disappoint my mother any more than I already have... I stop. A bronze hippie statue stands at the street corner and reminds me of The Eagles' song: "Standin' on the Corner..." I don't know anything anymore, I'm so tired. I lean against him. "Milena," he says, "Now listen to me. In two weeks you'll turn fifty. If you don't start living your life now, then when? Do you want to end up like me?"

That I don't want. I go back to the hotel where my keys await me at the reception.

The next day I drive back to Santa Fe from the south, from Albuquerque. Already the barren landscape, reddish rocks, silvery shrubs, the clear light, is familiar. The way the road rises, completely straight into the middle of the next mountain range, then across the plateau. Somewhere way out in the hills the red and yellow painted Rail Runner, the commuter train between Santa Fe and Albuquerque, glistens. My train. My hills. My light. A strange peace settles in me after all the excitement of the last few days. I'm here. Something will happen. From afar I see the green Starbucks mermaid that had already lured me on my first arrival. This time I have time. I take the exit, drink, eat, go to the drugstore, dawdle for an hour in the aisles and buy lots of things I don't need, shampoo, facial masks and hair scrunchies. The young woman at the register asks where I'm from and where I'm going.

"Santa Fe," I say.

"You live there? Or are you on vacation?"

"I don't know yet," I answer honestly.

She shrugs as if she's heard that often. "Santa Fe," she says, "how lovely." She'd never been there, she says, though she's lived here all her life, only thirty miles away. Santa Fe is more exotic for her than for me. I get another glimpse of the gulf that separates the rich and the poor, especially here.

I continue on, towards my fate. I pass Katchie's exit and drive on into town. When I exit the freeway I turn the wrong way onto Saint Francis Boulevard's three lanes. The rows of cars thunder towards me; I save myself by backing onto the freeway in reverse. My heart hammers in my throat, my hands tremble, behind me cars honk. I turn around and continue on, very slowly. It takes a long time till I calm down. I had reserved a room in a motel at the edge of town. There's a swimming pool but in the end I don't use it at all. The room faces directly onto the parking lot. I can't imagine I'll be comfortable here. It's hot.

I shower. Then I call Frederic. "I'm here," I say. I pull on a yellow dress and get going. When I get out of the car I'm trembling. There's Frederic. I look past his shoulder to the house. The door is open. I know immediately:

It is the House

Frederic offers me a drink, talks about the past weekend when he had an open house and how exhausting it was. But a real estate shark from Texas, who already owns the house next door, showed interest. He wants to consolidate the two houses. In other words: tear it down. "I would be very sorry about that." He again asks why I didn't get a loan. "It just doesn't make any sense. I have friends from Sweden ..." I interrupt him. "Let me tell you a story!" On the road I talked to myself. I visualized the whole scenario. After all, that's my profession: I tell stories. And so I tell Frederic how I Googled him and then asked my brother for a loan and finished with the words, "Now I can buy the house." The punch line has the expected effect: Frederic nearly spits out his drink. He jumps up, opens his arms and lets them fall again. He doesn't know what to say. "Don't you want to look at it again?" I shake my head. Not necessary. We sit on the comfortable easy chairs in the yard and it already feels like he is visiting me.

He calls George to give him the good news. George pencils me in for the next morning to fill out the paperwork. "Oh, I guess I better call Katchie's real estate agent Lisa," I say.

"Why would you do that?" Frederic asks. "You end up paying extra. You can trust George."

"OK," I say and put my phone away. Later Katchie tells me, "They always say that! It's not true. But if you have your own agent they'll have to share the commission." She will be annoyed many more times that she wasn't there to protect me from myself. But I am alone and I move forward in my own way, intuitive and trusting. Because I still am: full of trust.

"We should celebrate," Frederic says and jumps up. We walk down Canyon Road. I recognize the galleries Katchie and I visited and already I look at them with different eyes. Not with those of a tourist secretly worried that she'll be ripped off, but with the eyes of a neighbor who knows that we all have to survive somehow. Frederic shows me his first apartment in Santa Fe, a few houses away, and his artist's residence where he'll have an atelier and an apartment in July. "How does it feel to leave your house?" I ask. Somehow I sense that his departure is not completely voluntary.

"Santa Fe is a place to reinvent yourself," he says. "I had hoped somehow that I would do more art here, simply because I was so close and surrounded by all of it..." Instead he works for family services. Recently the government released a study on children and adolescents. New Mexico came in last place, and within New Mexico, Santa Fe County comes out the worst in most areas: poverty, child abuse, violence, graduation rates, teen pregnancy, drugs, alcohol... The situation is precarious. Not in the Appalachia's, not in the Bayous of Louisiana, but precisely here where multi-millionaires and film stars have their second houses? Second homes, that's it. During the summer months and around Christmas the population soars from eighty thousand to three hundred and sixty thousand. The part-timers bring money but they're not interested in the infrastructure. Their children don't go to school here. The politics don't concern them.

In San Francisco this voyeur status, this reporter position, bothered me after a while. I wanted to be part of the community I lived in. I wanted to contribute. Will this be possible here? Will I even be able to live here? Like other important questions, I cannot answer this one. Not yet.

"The government sent two agents who follow us around and watch us work," Frederic says. "We call them the Feds. One might say: panic reigns."

Even after his move to the artist's residence he will continue to work for the department of child services. Every resident is required to have two exhibitions a year. The first one is scheduled for six months after his move. "I'll be forced to draw again," Frederic says. "Even though I can't quit my day job, yet. What was your question?"

"Whether you won't find it hard to leave your house?"

"Hmm, honestly?"

"Yes, please."

"If I hadn't gotten this chance it probably would've been more difficult," he says, "but I'm on this seven year rhythm, seven years in New York, seven years in Santa Fe."

But you'll still be living in Santa Fe, I think to myself. We walk down Canyon Road, turn onto Delgado Street at Nathalie's boutique, cross the Santa Fe river which is completely dry. The neighborhood already feels familiar. I see myself walking these streets somewhere in the future – once I live here? My life is planned out years in advance with workshops, performances and book tours. My younger son is still in school. When you buy a vacation home you at least need to consider actually having vacations. On the other side of the world? And still, these paths are already familiar. Even before walking them more than once.

Finally we land in the garden of a Posada – another Posada, literally a place to sit and rest. This one's very different from the one in Winslow. A luxury hotel. The guests are stylish in the way Americans are, always a bit strained, a bit too formal. Frederic and I don't fit, he's wearing shorts, and I a wrinkled dress. It's nice not to be eating alone. In the background a musician plays the guitar. Suddenly the music grabs my attention. He sings "Don't Fence Me In." That's my song! The first song I ever performed. On stage, no less. Though there's nothing I fear more than singing.

Oh, wait: Spiders. But that fear I have faced. Three years ago I signed up for a seminar 'Fear of Spiders' at the Zurich Zoo. The fear of spiders had disrupted my life since I was very small. I could never enter a room without checking the corners. I have spent half a day in a room staring at the door frame where a big fat spider sat, unable to go through or to stop looking. I've regularly dreamed of eight hairy legs traipsing over my face, getting caught in my mouth and woken up in a panic. My world map had large white splotches. Wherever there were large spiders I could not go.

The course was being taught by a spider expert and a psychologist. The announcement that Sophie the red-kneed Mexican tarantula was waiting for us next door in a covered terrarium made me so nervous I could barely listen. Again and again my eyes traveled to the closed door. My heart beat irregularly to the rhythm of an Ernst Jandl poem: *"O o Sophie so viel Vieh o Sophie..."*

The psychologist advised us to pay attention and hold on to our physical reactions. As I looked at a picture of a spider, touched it, and finally had it projected onto my hand, my heart sped up, my hands went numb, I broke out in a cold sweat. But it all passed. Every time. During the lectures some of the unquestionable fascination of the expert transferred onto me. Spiders, I learned, carry their hearts in their rears. Less like a muscle and more like a soft bag, wrapped protectively around all the other vital organs, inadequately protected by thin skin. That touched me. Strangely. How brave, and how crazy, not to wear your heart on your sleeve but in your rear. And right away I stuck out my finger to touch Sophie's molted skin that felt surprisingly silky and soft.

The lifelong fear of spiders carved a groove in my brain that won't grow back. But, and that is the good news: I can lay down a new groove. By having a "positive experience" with a spider. Positive experience?

When Sophie reached out her long legs for my hand, I couldn't get any air. "Hang in there," said the psychologist. If I were to reach my goal of surviving the day I'd better keep breathing. One after another Sophie set her smooth feet onto my skin, a tiny tapping, and suddenly it happened, that which I could've never thought possible: I found her beautiful.

And then? What did I gain from it? I wasn't planning any marches through the rain forest. I didn't acquire any eight-legged pets. I continue living as before, only with one less fear.

One less fear? What that meant I only realized in time. The psychologist spoke of grooves in the brain. He compared them to a freeway that had been shut down. The longer it's unused the more nature takes over until it's hardly visible. While, a few kilometers away a new groove is made, a new road built. And the longer that one is being used the less one remembers there was once another one. But it's still there, just buried under weeds.

An autobahn needs space. That means my brain is large. That means I can build any connections I want, can make tracks, footpaths, blue highways, freeways. Nothing has to remain the same. I – as I see myself, as I define myself – don't have to remain the same. Everything is possible.

That I leave my husband, for the third time, and for good. And also that, a year later, I stand on a stage and sing. I fought against it until the very end. "I can't do that," I say. "I can't sing!" But I had picked this song "Don't Fence Me In" as the final number. I wanted to superimpose a Swiss translation, read it like a poem. Sybille was supposed to sing it. After all, she's the musician. But the director insisted. Under deathly torment, so I felt, I squeaked, "Oh, give me land, lots of land..." And my voice gave out, I broke off in shame. But the director didn't give up. "Louder!" she shouted, "Again!" Over and over. "Sing off key! As loud as you can."

Until I finally opened my mouth and yelled tearfully, "Don't Fence Me In!"

I have faced so many fears in recent years. Leaped so many seemingly insurmountable hurdles. Jumped so often into the void. And still, now that I sit on this patio raising a toast to a house purchase, first off I think: what will my mother say? She was so happy it didn't work out. I didn't tell her that I was driving to Santa Fe once more to look at the house. Because it could've turned out it wasn't the house. But the town. Or the man. Or none of the above. But now I'll have to tell her.

"That's my song," I tell Frederic. We chat like old friends. He asks about my work. "Tell me about your first book," he says. And I tell, and at some point, embarrassed, fall silent. My work as a writer forces me to talk about myself enough. In private, I prefer to listen. "And then?" Frederic continues. "What happened with your second book?" When I keep silent, he says, " I Googled you. You've written a whole bunch of books. So, come on, tell. The second? The third?"

I squirm and deflect. But a smile remains. I still smile when I get back into the car at his – my – house and he hands me a bottle of water.

"So you won't get dehydrated on the way." The desert climate needs getting used to, as well as the altitude of seventy-five hundred feet above sea level. His caring touches me. I still smile as I arrive at the motel. I think this is the beginning of a wonderful friendship.

Alone in Santa Fe

The next day I go to George's office and sign the offer. Instinctively I don't go far below the asking price. Frederic promised to leave all the furnishings. Which means I get a fully furnished house. A nicely decorated one no less. "Let's see what happens," George says. "I've gotten to know Frederic a bit. He may well change his mind."

It's strange to be alone in this moment. To have nobody there with me who is interested or more precisely, nobody who shares my excitement. I walk to the Plaza and sit on a bench in the park. In the pavilion a band is setting up. During the summer months, nearly every day there are free concerts here, from the afternoon into the evening. The regulars meet up, set up their camping chairs in respectful distance from the stage. In front, there's a half circle for couples to dance. Most of them have gray hair. They wear sensible shoes. In fascination I watch an elderly man who performs an amazingly nimble and weightless Salsa – in old Crocs. A woman with short silver hair wears hot pants and an undershirt, another blue leotards covered in shimmery sequins. The newspaper reported recently this was the best place to lose all inhibitions. Unnoticed I step from foot to foot. One day I will dance. Someday, somewhere, with someone. Or with myself.

I look around. No one except for me seems to be out alone. I know that's not true. Yesterday I didn't feel like that. Reality hasn't changed overnight, my perceptions have. I have bought a house. I live here now. At least for the moment. Traveling alone is different from living alone. Now, in this moment, with all my heart, I wish someone were here. Someone I could share it with. Someone to toast with. Someone who would be happy with me.

There is something unreal about this: a conference room in a real estate office. George offers me a glass of water. I sign, that's it. Five minutes later, I am back on the street. I have bought a house! Do I really have it if no one knows about it?

It's not official yet. Escrow takes thirty days. During that time an independent inspection happens, potential structural damage is discovered, the price is adjusted, there are discussions as to who'll be responsible for repairs. At the same time my finances are checked. I have to show a bank statement. My brother had the money transferred. My account is full to bursting.

I move from the motel at the edge of town to an expensive hotel on the Plaza. It is a gift to myself. I'm celebrating by myself. When I arrive to the hotel in my rental car an elderly man stands by the door looking out. I drive past him into the garage, park my car, take out my small suitcase and carry it to reception. "Oh, it's you, Milena!" the receptionist calls out. "Manolo, she's here!" The old man at the door turns and says, almost reproachfully, "I've been waiting for you."

"She snuck right past you," the receptionist jokes.

I get tears in my eyes. Someone was waiting for me, a pressed nose against the window glass, worried about me even. Does it take so little? Is that what I'm missing, someone waiting for me? Be careful what you wish for, I think. Your wishes might come true. For years I've been yearning for this very freedom. Not to be accountable to anyone. To disappear in a mass. It doesn't feel half as good as I thought it would.

"Are you here on business?" the receptionist asks.

"Not really..." Impulsively I tell these two men everything about the house I bought. They are very responsive. In the coming days they keep asking me about the state of things, help me with the paperwork, are happy for me. Soon the whole staff is involved with my house purchase. I am not half as alone as I thought.

Manolo carries my suitcase. I feel embarrassed. He's old and bent over; he only reaches up to my shoulder. I have a wonderful large room with a beautiful bath. Nothing else. There is no pool, no Wellness Center, nothing. It doesn't matter. Again I'm the only one traveling alone. Eating dinner, sitting at the bar. But the whole staff knows my story. And I know their names. I feel I belong. But to what? I don't know yet.

The first evening there's a thunderstorm that knocks out the electricity in the entire downtown. There are often thunderstorms in the summer, almost daily. The sky turns dramatically black, changes suddenly from bright blue to dark purple. Lightning flashes horizontally, fat raindrops sizzle on hot asphalt, turning to steam. It's called the monsoon season – even though the rain doesn't usually last more than ten minutes. The Santa Fe River that runs along the edge of downtown is dry. This evening the thunderstorm strikes. I sit at the bar by myself when the lights go out. I had just been trying to guess the names of a particularly festive group of people in the corner. They are actors in the TV series *Longmire* which actually takes place in Wyoming but is being filmed here. Santa Fe offers tax breaks to film and TV producers. Thus, much is being filmed here. And many actors, directors and producers live here. During filming they fall in love with the city, the landscape, the light. They buy a house – then the next role, the next film calls. Many unbelievably beautiful villas and ranches stand empty.

Lightning and thunder, then it all goes dark. The whole town is dark. A moment of silence, then everyone talks at the same time, too loudly. I stay on my stool. I have disappeared, swallowed by the dark. I no longer exist. Like a child who hides by covering her eyes. I suppress a giggle: that is freedom. No one knows who I am. Or where I am. At the next moment the waiter is standing at my side with a flashlight. The drink is on the house, he says, and "may I accompany you to your room?"

In my room there is a light stick on my bed. Before I fall asleep I watch a new film clip from Frederic. He forgot to charge his cell phone and without electricity... "In case we don't hear from each other anymore, dear friend, it was lovely!" He laughs. At this moment the light comes back on.

The next morning George calls, "Frederic rejected your offer."

"What?" I didn't expect that. "Why?"

"He asked me to be honest with you. He needs at least three hundred and eighty-five thousand to be able to pay off his debts."

"Oh, ah. OK." Still ten thousand below the original asking price. If Katchie were here she would remind me to get a second opinion, to stay tough. But she's not here and so I give in. I go by George's office again. In the meantime I've learned my way around the inner city quite well. I sign a new offer and we agree on a date for the inspection. Frederic responds rather offhandedly when I remind him that he promised to be out of the house by July 1st so that I could spend the last few weeks of my trip there. I begin to see that I can't take everything he says as gospel. I can't depend on anything.

George calls again. There is a problem with my bank account. "What's that supposed to mean?" I am becoming a bit hysterical. "This can't be true. If things go wrong now I have upset my mother for nothing!"

"Well..." George, a good fifteen years younger than I am, has no answer to that. And suddenly I see myself from the outside: a fifty-year-old woman, a successful writer, about to buy a house – who is afraid of disappointing her mother. I take a deep breath and let it out. "Sorry about that," I say. You can go far with an apology in America. Maybe that's what I like here:

no one is afraid of admitting a mistake. How honestly it is meant, particularly by politicians, is another question. But it simplifies the everyday, the social interactions, when everybody is ready, in principle, to say "my bad, sorry."

"So what's the problem?" I ask, more relaxed now. It turns out to be quite simple. The statement I copied from ebanking shows only half of the form. I take my laptop to the receptionist and ask the young woman who is working there today if she could help.

"Oh, so the sale is still on?" She seems to know all about it. I chat with her while she takes a screenshot. I thank her profusely. She looks at me sternly, "Should I show it to you once more? So you can do it yourself in the future?"

"Oh, yes. Thank you."

"No problem. I always have to explain everything to my mother several times, too."

Over the next few days I discover the city all by myself, spending lots of money on meals, on opera tickets. Frederic still sends me links to restaurants, to shoe stores with sales, to a Japanese bath high up in the hills. I keep asking myself what it is that fulfills me in this city. Mostly it's the views that take my breath away. The landscape. Not the town itself. I walk up to Cross of the Martyrs because I read in the newspaper that it's the best place to feel sorry for oneself – and to find the love of one's life. Neither happens, but I have an incredible view of the whole city.

From here I can also see how the town grew. The adobe architecture of the Pueblo was only re-discovered at the beginning of the twentieth century. By five artists who simply called themselves Los Cinco Pintores, but who were soon known as the Mud Hut Nuts, the adobe nuts. They correctly discerned that the traditional method of construction withstood the high desert climate better than any modern architecture. The sometimes meter-thick mud walls kept out the cold as well as the heat. So, while modern brick houses were being built on Palace Avenue, the artists laid out mud bricks to dry on their land on the Camino Monte del Sol, commonly known simply as the Camino, as though there were no others in the city. The writer Mary Austin, who moved to Santa Fe in 1924 after a nervous breakdown, was asked by a visitor if she could show her "Nut Row." "You know, the road where those crazies build their mud huts!" Thus the name Mud Hut Nuts. Then Mary Austin had them build her an adobe, her very own Casa Querida, her "beloved house." It took years for those houses to be built, and they still stand, indestructible. That was the beginning of the Adobe-fever. Soon all the influential high-society wives wanted such a house, until the whole town was covered with a layer of mud. The Mud Hut Nuts won.

I don't particularly care for the famous adobe architecture. From up here the town looks like an anthill. Like a Waldorf School fantasy. But a few days later I visit the New Mexico Museum of Art. I stand in the sculpture garden; I lay my head back and look up at the bright blue sky in perfect contrast to the dark wood beams and the ochre walls. I see it for the first time: it's beautiful. It is really beautiful. I have to laugh at myself. Most people fall in love with a city and then decide to move there. I only got the adobe-fever after the fact.

I can't say what it is. The landscape, the light, the crisp thin air, all that and more. Maybe it's what Paul Horgan in the *Centuries of Santa Fe* articulates: "Some attributed it to the high altitude air, some to the light, the colors overall. But above all something else could be felt. There was a hint of freedom of behavior, not in an immoral or indecent way but rather as a possibility of the individual to live his life in free expression. In these modern times maybe that was the most significant attraction of Santa Fe."

To live my life the way that was right for me. That is exactly what I've been looking for. That is happiness. And obviously it's no accident that I found this "hint of possibility" here. Every day I feel more at home here. I can be alone again without feeling bad about it. But enjoying it instead. I feel like something inside of me is waking up. I love the feel of the warm dry air on my skin. I love walking the dusty roads. I now see a slightly different version of myself, as in a cracked mirror, a bit older, a bit farther along. A woman who sits in a garden chair under a brightly colored sunshade and writes in a notebook. A woman who plants a narrow strip of garden around the seating area. Lavender and chamomile, and maybe something that can climb up the rough wooden fence. A woman who makes a fire in the fireplace, who sits in the window seat and reads. A woman who steps outside at night, tilts her head back and who has the whole sky with all the stars above her.

The Inspection

We meet at the house that I already consider my own. George is already there, the inspector as well. "Am I late?" I ask.

"No, no, everything's fine!" Here, too, I miss Katchie who later analyzes, "They discussed this before you arrived." Or her husband Joshua who says, "If anyone shows up early for a meeting in New Mexico, something's not right."

I'm not suspecting anything bad. I talk with Marco, the inspector, who originally came from Mallorca. We exchange the usual Europe vs. America anecdotes and observations. Everybody is so nice here. Marco opens the lid to the feared crawl space. Here very few houses have real basements or foundations, rather – in the best case scenario – they have a foot or two of space between the floor and the ground. Once, in San Francisco, when I had decided to remove the horrible linoleum from the bathroom floor, a corner of it came loose and when I pulled it I nearly fell backwards – six inches from me there was naked soil. Quickly I covered the hole and called a handyman who reassured me: , "That's totally normal, what did you expect?" Into this crawl space you can, if necessary, as the name suggests, crawl. In San Francisco I did exactly that, later on, when the pilot light for the gas heater went out. I feared such excursions not merely for the spiders that lived between those thin wooden beams. The whole construction seemed dangerous to me. My whole house rests on these toothpicks? Each time, I pulled a hood tightly around my head and tried to forget that the house could collapse on me. "You have to excuse me," Marco says now, "but I won't go under there. I'm simply too fat. I'll shine the flashlight if that's alright." Of course that's alright with me. Such a nice man. I wouldn't want him to get stuck in the opening! At this point in my narrative, Katchie is going to yell: "Milena! An inspector who doesn't check out the crawl space hasn't done an inspection! Why did you accept this?"

Yes, why? Maybe because I already knew I was going to buy the house no matter what? George had warned me, "Frederic has absolutely no money." So if the inspection revealed largish damages he wouldn't have any means of repairing them. Nor of lowering the price. "But you could just step back from the sale without losing your good faith money." So I sign another piece of paper, an addendum. I buy the house "as is."

When she hears about that, Katchie buries her head in her hands. "That guy was desperate! Of course he would've come down on the price." The house had been on the market for seven months, I only realize much later. Of course, Katchie is right. Katchie will be right later as well. I don't know that yet. I just know that I love the house. That it is my home. As is.

The inspection is supposed to last for a couple of hours. I'm not allowed to be there. Again I go to the Teahouse – I don't live here yet but already have my regular cafe. I order a real American breakfast with eggs and bacon but can't eat a bite. As I return from the cafe the two men are sitting together again. "The inspection went very well," Marco says. "I was surprised myself what good shape the house is in." The only complaint is the window in the bathroom which doesn't fulfill the requirements, and which some time in the future, will have to be replaced. Plus the roof will have to be cleared of leaves. That's all. I'm surprised. I was sure the roof was going to be a problem. No, the roof is fine. "The house is more than a hundred years old and in better shape than many newer ones," says Marco. Now there's nothing in the way of the purchase.

Again this strange emptiness. Something so monumental happens and I can't tell anyone. I call my sons. The older one is a bit hung-over and reacts restrainedly. Later he calls back. "I was taken by surprise," he says, "I'm sorry." I understand. "Me, too," I say. One after another the locations of his childhood disappear. The younger one is so polite it hurts. "If that is what you want, I'm happy for you." Obviously I'm not the only one who understands what this means: I'm starting a new life. My life. At least a different one. The others realize that too and feel that I'm moving away.

I had thought about remaining here until my birthday but I was slowly running out of money. More nights in the hotel, more restaurant meals – it won't last. Instead I drive back to California and spend a few extra days with Lil. At least now someone is happy for me. She doesn't understand how disappointed I am at the reaction of my sons, of other friends.

"Why do you need that?" she asks. "Are your decisions dependent on the reactions of others?"

"Of course they are!" I pause. Isn't that normal? Isn't that how it is for everyone?

"That's a completely unrealistic expectation," says Lil. "Just think about it."

I try. Of course it would be nice if my sons could be happy for me. But that's just not the way it is. If I make my decisions dependent upon their approval I can't live my life. It's that simple. And that hard. Only now do I begin to see how apprehensive I am of disappointing those close to me. And how much effort it takes me every time I try to please them.

Suddenly I remember a time when my younger son, Cyril, was little. He didn't sleep through a single night the first four years of his life. How often did I get up, zombie-like, desperate. Just once more, I think. If I go to him just this one time then he'll stay asleep. Of course it doesn't work and every marriage counselor, every hobby psychologist, can confirm that. I merely reinforced his behavior. Still, we all survived and now sleep wonderfully, thank you very much.

I now begin to see how this 'just once more' determined my behavior in my private life. I'll take this once more, I'll stay silent just one more time, I give in, just once more I'll do what you want – and the reward has to come! You will do it my way next time! You'll tell me, show me, how much you appreciate my sacrifice! Only, that can't be the driving force. To sacrifice oneself, to subvert one's own wishes, has to be done without expectation of reward.

An In-between Stop: Alice and David

"Santa Fe?" Alice shouts, "You're moving to Santa Fe?" Alice was my first yoga instructor in San Francisco and one of my best friends. The closeness between us remained even though we rarely see each other anymore and no longer keep track of our daily lives. Some relationships don't depend on external circumstances. Whenever we meet we start right where we left off. But now she doesn't understand me. She makes a face as though suppressing a smirk when she says 'Santa Fe.' "Are you going to wear clunky turquoise jewelry from now on?" she asks. "Will you be painting sunsets?" Just as my Zurich friends asked whether I would begin wearing white ankle socks when I moved to the Canton Aargau. In San Francisco, too, no one shares my enthusiasm for my – admittedly sudden – decision. It takes me a while to understand that my friends are hurt. I come back, but not to them. Exactly like my Swiss friends, they feel I am abandoning them. I am deciding against them. Against the place where we could all be together. Voluntary emigration is a decision that has to be borne alone. It's not possible to blame the job, the husband. You have to take the responsibility, absorb the reactions.

But then Alice shows me a newspaper clipping. "Why didn't you say so right away? Now it's become clear!"

"What? Show me!" Armistead Maupin moved to Santa Fe! As if I needed another sign. The author of the cult series *Tales of the City* was the reason I wanted to move to San Francisco in the first place. I read the six volumes during my pregnancy, one after the other. They appeared originally as a serialized novel in the newspaper, the characters dangling from cliff hanger to cliff hanger. I identified right away with Mary Ann Singleton who arrived in San Francisco and knew immediately: this is my city. This is where I belong. I remember thinking me too! That's exactly how I feel. Even though I'd never been to San Francisco. I held a four-day-old baby in my arms and my older son had just started first grade. Nothing was further from our horizons than moving abroad. Some years later, when I actually lived in San Francisco, I wrote to Armistead Maupin and told him the story. He never replied. He probably gets letters like that daily. Armistead Maupin is a living symbol of San Francisco. He embodies the soul of the city like no other.

Armistead Maupin left San Francisco. Armistead Maupin now lives with his husband in Santa Fe. "We just wanted a garden for our dog," the official explanation says. "Then it got really out of hand—we ended up with 15 acres full of coyotes." And a house a size they could no longer have afforded in San Francisco. "Writers are notoriously underpaid."

"Oh, well," Alice says. "I understand. So be it. At least it's closer than Switzerland."

"How the hell did you come up with Santa Fe?" asks David, her husband. His arms are full of toys as it's time to put the two girls to bed.

"I just wanted to visit some happy couples..."

"And you didn't come here first?" David grins in my direction, but his eyes seek Alice. They exchange a look above my head. A look I have learned to recognize. All the couples I've visited share it. I know you, it says. I know who you are and I'm glad you exist.

"But I'm here now," I say to him. When he met Alice about twelve years ago she, a yoga instructor in her mid-thirties, had given up on love. She lived ascetically, was a strict Vegan, got up daily at 4:00 AM to meditate and practice. Then along came David. He was younger than she was, a furniture maker and workshop teacher with a twirled mustache. Today one might call him a hipster. He ate hardly anything other than meat, performed with his band until the early mornings and generally treated every get-together as a costume party. He was as flamboyant as she was disciplined. "We are going to get married," Alice said after the first date that, because they couldn't find a restaurant that was amenable to both their eating habits, took place inside her van. They sat up all night smoking self-rolled cigarettes and talking until seven in the morning. "He'll be the father of my kids."

It all went much faster than could have imagined. I was there when Alice took her first pregnancy test. I was the matron of honor at her wedding, a role I seriously underestimated despite all the movies I had seen. "A speech? I have to give a speech?" At the birth of her first baby, I was there. I spent twenty-four hours in the hospital, mostly in the waiting room that we shared with a large Mexican family. Every forty-five minutes we switched the TV from an English speaking channel to a Spanish speaking one. Alice's parents had arrived from Los Angeles. At some point Alice's mother fell asleep in her chair and I ended up talking with Alice's father who she was very close to. He was a wonderful, insightful and loyal man, the kind of father I always wanted. I still remember how we talked about the state of my marriage, how I asked him for advice. "I think you're driven by shame," he said. "You'd feel so ashamed if this marriage failed too, that you let yourself in for a pretty absurd arrangement..." I was shocked. I didn't really want to know that clearly. But I never forgot his words – even though it would be years before I found the courage to act upon them.

Alice and David don't have much money and hardly any time for each other. He works days, she evenings and weekends. Clearly they have a lot on their plate, what with raising two beautiful, very unique girls. A situation that is of course very common. So often the burden becomes too much and couples, even loving ones, turn against each other. One of the low points of my marriage was when I colored in the weeks that we stayed home to take care of the kids, in different colors.

"46 weeks are green!" I yelled, "and only 6 red! Look at that!" I was also the main breadwinner for the family, taking on both traditional roles. That was what Alice's father called an absurd arrangement. I remember the resentment still. I see it in many couples who try to juggle family and work. Who does more? And why? And how is that fair? But not here. Alice and David communicate without many words. They don't think about their own workload as much as they attempt to ease each other's lives. In the mornings they both get up an hour early to drink coffee together. "It's the best time of day," he says.

"I look forward to it even in my sleep," she says.

And so now I'm here with David and Alice in Oakland, twenty minutes from San Francisco. I decide to spend the night. The house is very small and David made all the furniture himself. In his workshop the girls have their own work spaces where they work on their projects. In the huge, romantically overgrown garden lives a three legged turtle. It's so beautiful it hurts. It makes me miss something I never had.

David comes back from the children's bedroom, opens a bottle of wine and we settle on the stoop, talking. I tell them about the couples I've stayed with. The house I fell in love with. The sky above New Mexico.

"What you've seen with those couples you visited, that is friendship," says my wise friend Alice. "It's not about falling in love, it's about friendship."

Friendship? How so – why not love? My inner-romantic rises from her sickbed and drops her white frilly dress. Underneath she wears jeans. She smiles at me with a friendliness I don't deserve.

"Stop already with all that self-flagellation," she says. "Friendship begins with yourself." Playfully she wags a finger. I don't know this high-spirited self. Now she even laughs. That night while brushing my teeth I look at myself in the mirror, differently. Suddenly I recognize this look. It says: There you are! Good to see you. I'm sure glad you exist!

Fifty is the New Fifty

In San Francisco I rented an apartment for two weeks. A beautiful, large, well-furnished apartment with a deck, in the middle of the Castro. The apartment is big enough for a party, if I want to have one. And for my sons if they want to stay over. They both come. They're both here.

I didn't expect that. Lino didn't know until the last minute if he could make it. For Cyril, on the other hand, it's the last summer to visit his friends in San Francisco before they scatter all across the country for college. Most of my friends have become empty-nesters in one fell swoop. I'm in a strange mood, between euphoria and panic. "The transitions are hardest," I suddenly remember. I think it was Lino's first kindergarten teacher who told me that years ago, trying to comfort me as I left my crying child. He, who at the end of the day, didn't want to leave any more. I understood. At home it's good, playgroup is good. It's only the transition that is not.

My friend and stage partner Sibylle arrived from Switzerland. She'll stay for a week before traveling on to Louisiana, to see Susanne and Doug whom she knows much better than I do. A week before my birthday I still don't know how I want to celebrate it. In the last ten years the event had lost its significance. When I was younger I went to great lengths to celebrate properly. Maybe because it falls during summer vacation and I therefore could not have a party as a child? But my fortieth, the party my friend Pie threw for me, was set in her garden with a desert tent with gold poles, Egyptian clothing and a lawn covered with Oriental rugs, an incredible buffet, music and all the people I used to know back in Switzerland… That party satisfied my birthday wishes for good. Since then I celebrate in a haphazard way. But my forty-fifth was lovely, too, I remember now. I was by myself in our dream house and did what I like to do most: I invited everyone I knew, friends and family, the neighbors from the village and friends from Zurich. The most diverse group of people who would usually never sit together and who suddenly realized they have more in common than just knowing me. I still remember that Katchie, who happened to be in Switzerland, helped me bake traditional ham croissants all morning (I had recently been given a croissant maker and didn't want to eat anything else, ever). My former father-in-law manned the bar, my neighbors made friends with my editor, and at the end, all the remaining and half-way sober women dug through my shoe closet. I had broken an ankle and was convinced I would never wear high heels again. The simplest parties are often the best. But that seems difficult for a fiftieth.

How many fiftieths have I witnessed in recent years? Mostly I got jittery after an hour and would leave. A fiftieth birthday always seems to have to prove something: See what I have achieved! Look how well I'm doing! See how great I look! How many friends I have!

"For that money I could've bought myself a car," a friend summed up a party I missed.

What do I have to show? At this particular point, nothing. Only that I know what's important: my sons, my friends. Every year, less of them live here.

In the end it's all very easy. I invite all the people I still know here. I order Thai food from a restaurant and have my nails painted dark blue. They match my dress I bought in Switzerland because the colors reminded me of the sky and earth in Santa Fe; it's an orange and blue pattern and vaguely Native American inspired. To be precise, it reminds me of the airport in Albuquerque.

Sibylle unwraps the present she gave me. A beautiful hand-stitched wall hanging she worked on for months. Richly decorated with birds and flower vines, and in beautiful script: "Die chönd mer all am Bürzi chnüüble" which would most closely translate as 'they can all kiss my butt.' It's a quaint, old-fashioned expression Sibylle uses frequently and it makes me laugh every time. The Bürzi is a bun and chnüüble means t. In short: let them use their superior attitude where it doesn't hurt me. I decide that should become my mantra for my next year.

I lay the "Bürzi," as I'll call it for short from then on, on my bed. In San Francisco, in Santa Fe, in Aarau. And because the "Bürzi" needs to lie flat for the message to be presented best, I'm forced to make my bed every day. And that, I find, is the best medicine against early morning listlessness and melancholy.

At five o'clock the first guests arrive. My former neighbor Jack is here. He unpacks his camera to take pictures. And he grills new potatoes from his garden with olive oil and herbs. Back when I lived in San Francisco he supplied me almost daily with fresh salad greens, radishes, green beans and potatoes. In return I drove him to the doctor, the pharmacy and the post office. Nearly every day on his way to the local store he stopped by and with these words, "I don't want to bother you, I know you're writing," he would introduce a twenty-minute conversation. "No, no, I don't want to come in," so he stood leaning on his walking stick in my doorway and explained the world to me. My only escape was the fact that the local store had senior discounts until three o'clock. "Jack, it's ten to three," I would say and shut the door on him.

The former engineer composed a limerick for me and printed it by hand in large letters on a brown paper roll. That "Young people these days don't learn proper script" is one of his pet peeves. He manages to corner Lino who's studying architecture and explains to him how important it is for architects to understand the work of the engineers, to trust them. Lino listens politely for a while until he escapes with an excuse. He's heard this speech often before. So have I. All of a sudden I, too, have a deja-vu: how many parties like this one have we had before?

Janet and Tom, whose son used to go to school with Lino, are there. For a while Lino spent so many weekends with them that he was listed as their son on the roster of their church. We haven't seen each other for years. First off I notice Janet has lost a lot of weight. "You look wonderful," I exclaim as if I didn't know that losing weight is not always deliberate or a good sign. Janet is a corporate lawyer. Her husband Tom is a programmer who's been unemployed for years. He wrote a book that explained in thousands of pages "how the universe works." I tried to read it but gave up after a hundred pages. The universe is too complicated for me and Tom's way of thinking too foreign. Deb remains unwavering by his side, "Isn't it wonderful? I'm so proud of him."

Now she too has lost her job. At nearly sixty her outlook is not good. During the years of juggling debit and credit cards more and more got cancelled. When you're unemployed, you don't have health insurance. That means you can't get sick. Whether Scott finds his way in 'real' life or Deb's fingers turn to claws from arthritis, it's their own problem. They gave up their spectacular apartment downtown and now live in a furnished room they pay for in cash. A week in advance, sometimes only a day. "Residential Hotels" they are called in San Francisco. They're primarily used by the homeless as a last resort. Most prefer sleeping in their cars, as long as they still can hang on to them. Janet and Tom don't own a car anymore. There isn't any money for food, some days.

"It's a spiritual experience," Tom says of the forced fasting. Janet drops her gaze. Ten years ago when our sons went to school together, that sweet couple took me under their wings. They made lots of money and spent lots. Once before, they had both been unemployed at the same time, at which time they took out another loan and sent their son to an expensive private school. Will this work? I wondered back then. But what do I know from about money?

Then I moved to Switzerland. My son studied for free there. Deb's son has to work and support his parents. For a moment I am glad to be living in Switzerland. In Switzerland one can't fall through the cracks this way. On the other hand, Switzerland has one of the highest suicide rates in the world. There must be other kinds of cracks.

Another friend, too, is not doing well. Her partner who owns the house they live in turns out to be an alcoholic. She doesn't make enough to leave him. She can't really afford San Francisco but it's where she grew up. She can't imagine living anywhere else. She stays too long; at one point she cries. "I don't know how this happened," she says. "Is this my life?" I know how she feels.

I think the City eats its children.

In one interview Armistead Maupin argued against the "everything used to be better" attitude that he deplored in his idol, the legendary Herb Caen. Caen who loved the City as completely as Maupin did and who – in very different words, but equally lastingly – built a memorial to the City, lamented in the seventies how much better the forties had been. Today Maupin fights the same temptation – to idolize the seventies, his time, when San Francisco was still San Francisco. "I'm feeling the same things San Franciscans are feeling: the astonishment and mild horror over the high-rises going up along Market Street. But I think a certain amount of acceptance about these things is necessary. Cities change, people change, the only thing that hasn't changed is the urge of young people to move to San Francisco. What's different now is some of them have a lot of money and can displace people who don't. It's very hard for artists to live in San Francisco anymore. But San Francisco will always be San Francisco," he writes.

The high tech and computer businesses of the Silicon Valley send white buses with spooky mirrored windows through the City collecting workers to take them down to the Peninsula. In the mornings, cafes at certain corners are crowded with geeky unfriendly young people who talk loudly into their invisible phones and who order complicated caffeinated drinks that are hard to pronounce and even harder to prepare. They toss money on the counter without counting or raising their gaze. They are young, they are important, they own the City. Then the bus rolls up silently, the cafes empty, the plague of locusts is gone. Till the early evening when the buses arrive again and spit them out. If you don't belong you get pushed aside.

I remember back in the late nineties I already felt exactly the same: I tried to buy a house and was booted out by kids in khakis and sneakers who, without blinking, paid double the asking price and added a few shares from their start-ups. Suddenly the menus of the best restaurants in town were aimed at youngsters: deep fried cheese sandwiches, artisan beer on tap. I already felt driven out of the City. Even more so when the then-mayor, flamboyant and corrupt Willie Brown, said in an interview that those who made less than sixty thousand a year did not belong here. This number has probably tripled by now.

"The City changes constantly," says my friend Theresa who grew up there. "Ever since I remember people have said "It's not like it used to be. It's no longer our San Francisco!" she shrugs. Even Darwin said, "it's not the strongest who survive but those who can adapt best."

"Easy for you to say," another interjects. "Your house is paid off. You're safe."

Lino brought along his roommate from Zurich, Aurel whom he's known since elementary school. Until today I'm still shocked to see their shoes by the front door, looking as big as row boats. I still see their first "big shoes" in front of me, shoes with laces, ready to be tied. It's Aurel's first time in California but he's so comfortable that everyone thinks he's been living here forever. He fits perfectly in this City that – all we have to do is think back – receives everyone with open arms. His enthusiasm is infectious.

Lino hands me his present: "For your new house!" It's a world map with pictures of himself and his brother that I had taken the evening before my departure. "Wherever we are, whatever we do, we are family," reads the inscription.

"You have to frame it of course," he says as he rolls it back up. Too late. I'm already crying.

Later on we sing on the deck outside. It's the only nice evening all week. No fog, almost summer temperature. Steiner, our first friend in San Francisco and the most important and long-time teacher of both boys, starts out "Happy Birthday." His voice fills the balmy evening air, he pulls us all along, even those who don't want to sing. Hundreds of memories flood in. It's almost like it used to be. How many parties have we had, on his, on our deck? How often have we let ourselves be pulled along by his voice singing "Happy Birthday" and "Oh, Tannenbaum" and everything in between? And now I understand what it is. Why I feel so strongly that this is no longer my city. It's not the Google buses, not the inflated prices, not the fact that so many of my friends have moved away. San Francisco was the city where I lived with my ex, where we built a new life as a family. Every street corner, every cafe, every park bench is full of memories.

My fiftieth ends with a call from the landlord. "Look, I'm sorry, I know it's your fiftieth, but... the neighbors called four times. They are complaining and threatening to call the police."

It's Saturday night shortly after ten o'clock in the middle of the wild Castro district, in the heart of the gay party scene, in the metropolis of San Francisco. We didn't dance or play music. Just sang a bit. In Aarau, center of Swiss provincialism, nothing like that ever happened to me. I have to laugh. It always feels good to get rid of certainties and prejudices.

The guests depart. I lie down on the bed and cover myself with the Bürzi. I am fifty years old. I have bought a house in Santa Fe. Against all reason and good intentions. But it feels as good and as right as anything has in a long time. Even if it isn't clear to anyone but me: they can all "nibble my bun."

At Home, Finally.

Shortly after my birthday I turn in my apartment and my rental car. I have barely two weeks before my sabbatical ends. This time I fly to Santa Fe. I don't want to lose a single day. Cyril comes along, good-naturedly leaving his friends for a few days. "It's important to me that you see it," I say and he gives in. At the airport in Albuquerque he has the same reaction I had. "It doesn't look like America," he says.

Cyril spent his formative years in America. That means his childhood differs from that of his brother's in countless ways, despite globalization. To begin with his childhood books: *Green Eggs and Ham*, rather than *Joggeli gaat go Birrli schuettle*. But mainly, Cyril had a childhood without Cowboys and Indians. Lino, after the dinosaur and whale phase, had a period of Indians. He devoured everything – except Federica de Cesco, "that's for girls" of course – he practically moved into the Native American museum in Zurich. He invested his pocket money in leather patches and beads and sowed his own moccasins. Once I was called in to school because in an essay about "things I need to be happy" he didn't write, like all the other students "my mom, my dad, my friends, God" but instead, "a time machine, a few friends, guns, and fast horses." At least friends were on his list, I thought. After the usual lead in – "you are a working mother, Mrs. Moser, you write those… hmmm… murder mysteries. How much time does your son spend in front of the TV by himself?" I suggested they let my son explain what he meant: saving the Indians from the arrival of Columbus.

In an American childhood none of this fits. The Natives are silenced. Only in school plays do they show up when, shortly before Thanksgiving, the children perform the scenes of the

Indians saving the settlers from starvation. Corn cobs are distributed, a paper mache turkey passed around. The part about the pox ridden blankets is left out.

And still Cyril reacts to the airport paintings and those on the overpasses on the road home. Stylized rabbits, ravens and coyotes interrupt the ornaments. "Those are totem animals," I try to explain but I don't know enough myself. I hear myself babble. "Oh, look at the sky. Isn't that gorgeous? You see that? Look at the mountains, the light!" I notice only after a while that Cyril is wearing his head phones.

We spend the first night at the hotel. This time at the Saint Francis, a huge former monastery with refreshingly austere rooms and humane prices. In the evening we eat at the bar, a green chili cheeseburger, a mixture of American and Mexican influence and a local specialty. Cyril declares it too spicy. I notice how tensely I watch him, how important it is for me that he like it here. I have to force myself to relax. He does not have to share my enthusiasm. It's enough that he is here. Outside streams of tourists stroll past on the way to the Plaza where there's music. A few notes reach us. We could make it to the house in ten minutes on foot but during the thirty day escrow I'm not allowed in. Has it only been a month since I sat in George's office and signed my offer? I keep looking at the pictures from my last visit. As if I have to reassure myself that the house exists. And belongs to me.

The next morning I am expected at George's office to sign over the land deed. Cyril meant to come along but when the alarm goes off I can't wake him. It doesn't matter because once again the process is anticlimactic and quickly completed. A few signatures, a bit of small talk, a glass of water. As soon as the money has been transferred from the escrow account to Frederic's account, I'll get the keys. It shouldn't take more than a couple of hours. I return to the hotel and wake Cyril. We eat breakfast; I keep checking my phone. Yesterday, as every day before, I had multiple messages from Frederic. Today, nothing. It feels strange. I have gotten used to the constant virtual presence. George texts, "All good. Keys in mailbox." We check out, carry our suitcases to the car and drive the short distance to the house. The mailbox is unlocked. The key chain reads: "I got ruined in New Mexico!"

Ha, ha! I text Frederic, "Good joke!" No response. In the fridge there's a bottle of champagne. In addition to the furniture and pictures, Frederic left me a few books. *Gardens in New Mexico, Santa Fe Style*. On the desk an empty notebook and a pen are ready for me. I am touched. How thoughtful. "What a nice reception," I text again. "Thank you." No response.

Cyril flops onto the window seat, plugs in his computer. There is no Internet and no TV in the house. Outside it's hot. There is no mattress on the bed. I could've thought of that. "Come on," I say to Cyril. "Time to go shopping." Reluctantly he heaves himself up. We need food, bed linens, silverware and plates. I promise a toaster oven to heat up pizza. I know this is not the kind of vacation a teenager wants. To sit in a car with his mom, to scour shopping centers. In contrast to the quaint downtown, the outlying areas are depressing. Four lane highways divide the endless expanse bordered by supermarkets and chain stores in adobe tan. Some are even shored up with fake beams imitating the traditional "zaguan." Even the drive-through cash machines are in the style of Pueblo architecture. The effect is at best irritating.

In the stores the Santa Fe style dominates: colorful, rustic, with Mexican influence. Patterned blankets, brightly colored metal ornaments, beaded lampshades, embroidered pillows, cow skulls often painted or covered with turquoise ornaments. Suddenly I don't think my house is perfectly furnished or doesn't need change. On the contrary, all that tan, brown and olive has to go, to be replaced by primary colors, by wild patterns. I buy bright Mexican blankets for the sofa and wildly patterned pillows. But I let Cyril pick the dishes; he chooses the simplest, in white. Later, every time I get a dish from the cupboard I feel a certain relief. They are an oasis of calm in the color storm I unleashed.

I buy all his favorite foods. Childhood memories: Apple Jacks cereal and Pizza Pouches, frozen pizza pockets. I remember how, in San Francisco, he peered into my pots and innocently asked what I was cooking, then disappeared. I didn't even notice he had left the house until he returned some ten minutes later and, all innocently, pulled out a package of Pizza Pouches from behind his back. "Look! I bought my own dinner! With my own money. So you won't have to bother so much with the cooking."

In San Francisco we also had a tree house, more of a wooden platform on the thickest branch of an old plum tree. Sometimes we ate up there. Long ago. Cyril is no longer a child. But he still loves Pizza Pouches. At the last moment I remember the oven. I buy an electric one and set it on the stove.

The mattress I have to order; it will take a week for delivery. So we both sleep in the living room, I on the sofa, he on the window seat. It's comfy. For a while our computer monitors glow. Shortly before midnight I can't stand it any longer and activate the roaming function on my cell phone to check my email. And there, finally, a message from Frederic. Though it's not addressed to me personally – I must have accidentally ended up on the receiver list. It's one of his video clips, showing him rather drunk in one of the best restaurants in town. "Did you hear?" he roars, "as of today I'm free of debt! Free! Cheers!" Shocked, I drop the phone. That will be the last time I hear from him for a while.

I begin to understand that he was indeed quite desperate to sell the house and needed money in the worst way. And still, I thought something more than a house sale connected us. After all, he remained in touch the whole time. Sent me numerous film clips, often wrote several times a day. Showed me the layout for an Internet magazine he was planning to start and offered me a column. "Your first column in English! Or do you know Spanish?" He invited me to visit him at work, to his favorite project: Resilience training for at risk teenagers in Espanola. I told Frederic about the program "School House Novel" that sends writers into classrooms. "You could start something like that here," he said. "I can help. I have contacts." He was going to show me the pueblos, he wanted to take a train trip with me. He was, so I thought, my first new friend in Santa Fe. The first one I had met independently of Katchie and Joshua. But the moment the money was in his account, he completely disappeared from my life. From one day to the next I heard nothing more.

That surprises me – but it doesn't make me mad. Why am I not angry? My girlfriends are. "He used you! He flirted with you so you'd buy his house!" True. But had he not flirted I might not have Googled him. Had I not Googled him I would not have had the impetus to ask my brother for money. Had my brother not lent me the money I couldn't have bought the house. And had I not bought the house I wouldn't be here now. And if I know nothing else, I know this: here I am at the right place. This is home. And if it's just the house, not the street, not the town, not the state, not the continent – it is enough. The house and the sky above.

Every morning we traipse to the Teahouse with our laptops to use the Internet. Then Cyril drops his iPhone. His only connection to the outside world is gone. The following days we comb the outlying shopping centers for a repair facility. No success. In one cafe somebody writes down a number. "Jack is, as far as I know, the only person who deals with Apple." – "Here? It's the third world," I keep hearing. In fact there are supposedly Americans who think New Mexico is South of the Border. "Don't you need a visa?" they ask. That, too, is a question the people from Zurich like to ask in connection with the Canton Aargau. But the Americans mean it. New Mexico was cut off from the rest of the United States for so long it hasn't quite caught up. The rhythm is different.

Almost from the moment the whites settled here, there have been two conflicting movements. The ones who want to modernize New Mexico and those who want to preserve it. The feeling of being stuck in history is precisely part of the attraction. At least for those who come here to retire. For the artists, the writers. But for those growing up here and raising children, it's frustrating.

The boom began in Santa Fe in the eighties. It was sparked by an outrageous lifestyle article in Esquire that declared the – then rather sleepy and secluded – artist oasis as being the Right Place. The Mecca for a new group, the yuppies, the Young Urban Professionals. They wore flashy watches and gelled their hair, they made and lost more money in a month on the stock market than their parents had earned their whole lives. They lived on cocaine and cappuccinos and stood out in the stark romantic landscape of New Mexico like a sore thumb. They came in hordes and bought whole tracts of land, plopped giant villas on top of hills. They did have to follow the conservancy regulations that, since 1957, required that all buildings look traditional. But the adobe structure loses its meaning when it surpasses a certain size. The relatively low prices seduced many to buy more land than they needed and to build bigger houses than they required. Like Armistead Maupin who wanted a garden for his dogs and now sits on fifteen acres of land. He, by the way, is back in San Francisco my friends tell me. His villa is for rent on Airbnb, five hundred and twenty dollars a night. "He got bored in Santa Fe," my friends report with a slightly smug undertone. "It seems there's nothing to do there." An assessment my son obviously shares.

Nothing to do – maybe. But there is something to be here: Oneself. A sensation that apparently requires a certain age.

The unintentional withdrawal from technology does not improve tempers. In order to repair the iPhone we have to drive to Albuquerque. "Not until tomorrow," I say, "on the way to the airport." I can see that Cyril can hardly wait for the end of these days of togetherness, just as I feared. I desperately want to show him something he'll remember fondly later. At least he enjoyed the Indonesian masks Frederic left behind. They scare me and I took them down and hid them in the kitchen cabinet. But Cyril loves them and plans to take them back to Switzerland to hang in his room.

Cyril is bored.

Then I remember the butch army officer I met on the plane. Was this really just one month ago? "What do you think of visiting an old mining town? Like in the Wild West?" Cyril shrugs. We drive off, half an hour South on Highway 14, the Turquoise Trail. The road that connects the mining towns of Madrid, Golden and Cerrillos with Santa Fe owes its name to an audience competition. The first prize, a suitcase set, presumably in turquoise, went to a teacher in Albuquerque. In fact, along this trail turquoise had been mined. The Pueblo has used the stone for religious artifacts since the year 900 AD. Particularly around Cerrillos, the "small hills," a particular type of turquoise, almost grass green, could be found. In Madrid, on the other hand (stress on the first syllable, as it was impressed upon me), coal was mined in the early nineteenth century, particularly for the railroad, the Santa Fe Railway. The end of the coal industry brought an end to the town as well, until, in the seventies, artists and craftsmen moved into the empty houses. Since then Madrid is known as being the place for dropouts and dissenters. Maybe because all those empty mine shafts create hollow spaces. Maybe because of a vortex of electromagnetic power lines. Maybe just because. It's a special place. Invisible from the road, in a slight dip between two hills, it appears like a mirage after a turn in the road. The corrugated iron roofs glitter in the sun. Here there's no adobe architecture. The tiny identical houses, with small porches and back doors, seem to have remained unchanged since the coal era.

To my relief, Cyril likes Madrid. We stroll up and down the short main street, dig through the offerings of thrift stores, buy a few things. An old blanket with a hole in the middle, a flower pot, a huge crucifix. Then we eat hamburgers at the Mine Shaft Tavern. Without green chilis. On the way home we are accompanied for a while by a bunch of bikers. They leave us in a cloud of dust. At the edge of town we see a herd of miniature horses galloping along the strip of burned grass, pursued by three men with lassos.

Now that, my son admits, you don't see anywhere else.

Enter the Captain: Connie and Magdalena

A few days later an RV stops at my door and Magdalena gets out. "I'm coming to see how you live." She brings Tibetan prayer flags and a tiny woolen lucky charm her girlfriend Connie knitted. Connie herself didn't come that time. The long drive in the RV was too much, they had just returned from a longish road trip. Connie is eighty-one.

When I met Magdalena she had just broken up with her partner. She knew exactly what she was looking for in the next one: she should be younger for sure "I've got enough trouble with aging," politically involved, a lesbian activist preferably, definitely no more women with heterosexual pasts. Sounds good, I thought. When I saw her next, she was head over heels in love with Connie, a Chinese woman eighteen years her senior, married for forty years to a man her parents had chosen for her. Magdalena is her second relationship – and her first great love. After the divorce Connie distracted her rage at her husband with varied activities, Mah Jong, playing the ukulele, knitting. And she joined Magdalena's writing group.

Magdalena is an author. She is the sister of Matthias and Adrian Zschokke, the other Kroesus Verlag author. I'd been living in San Francisco for several months when he told me he had a sister who lived very close, in Santa Cruz. "And you tell me that now?" He suggested I write about her, which I did. On assignment from a Swiss woman's magazine I called her. I spoke Swiss but she interrupted me, "I don't do that anymore!" Her relationship to the old country is fraught, at best. "I reinvented myself when I left," she said, "as someone who speaks English."

She was twenty-four when she flew to New Zealand for a semester abroad. She arrived three days later. "You see how long ago that was." The fact that she made it to the other end of the world made her bold. She took a job on a sailboat whose owner had lost his wife and needed someone to clean and paint. "I can do that," Magdalena coolly declared and as her first act dumped a gallon of paint in the ocean. But somehow the boat got ready and the owner asked if she wanted to be part of the crew to California.

"Sure!" It was her first time on a boat on the open ocean and for six months to boot. When she arrived in California they hadn't seen land for five weeks. She felt reborn. "I survived – I'm invincible – I want to do it again!" The semester abroad fell flat. Instead she spent twelve years at sea, mostly as a captain of charter boats, without permanent residence, always moving. "That's why I write in English. The world of sailing only exists for me in that language."

We made a date for the next weekend in Santa Cruz; the whole family took a trip down the coast. My then husband was supposed to take the pictures for the article. We would take turns playing with the kids on the beach and visit the Boardwalk, an old-fashioned funfair directly on the water with America's oldest roller coaster, the wooden Giant Dipper. Santa Cruz, South of San Francisco on the Pacific is the undisputed capital of surfers, hippies, eccentrics – and tourists on the weekends. On the Boardwalk every day is party day. Roller coaster, cotton candy, souvenir shops. A paradise for children – Santa Cruz will remain their favorite holiday destination. Here Magdalena got cleaned up after a terrible, ninety hour storm. "The waves were taller than the boat. I was no longer afraid, I just wanted it to be over. When we got here the sun was out and people were happily surfing, while we had nearly drowned out there. Totally surreal." Soon thereafter she quit sailing, not least because she figured she'd used up her luck. After the death of her father, Magdalena returned to Switzerland for a short while. Afterwards, somehow, sailing had lost its appeal. She looked for a university to continue her literature studies and landed again in Santa Cruz, the town she had washed up in years earlier. The university is known for its women's studies department and the town is at the ocean. Magdalena doesn't sail any longer but she goes boogie boarding. "Surfing for the untalented," she calls it lying on her belly on a short foam board and riding the breakers to shore. She doesn't miss life on the water. "Except, maybe, all those stimuli that flood us on land. After two or three weeks without, you see colors much more intensely, particularly the reds and yellows. And the smells!"

We made a date in a place typical for Santa Cruz in the nineties: Rebecca's Mighty Muffins. I remember Magdalena made fun of my breakfast habits. "They still do coffee in Europe?" she asked wryly. I also remember we ended up talking for seven hours and that I couldn't use any of it in my article. It was friendship at first glance.

When I met Magdalena she wrote short stories and mysteries. With a slight ironic undertone she spoke of THE great novel she would write. This she did with her most recent book *Diving the Wrecks.* With her main character, she plays through the life that would have awaited her had she stayed in Switzerland. A scary, depressing symphony of gray tones and varying degrees of cold, repeatedly opening into bright colorful visions. Visions of ocean, of sky, of fog, of waves breaking on beaches. Of the Boardwalk, of Santa Cruz, of another possible life. It is a book less written than borne. But Magdalena doesn't believe in the romantic ideal of the writer in the ivory tower. "It is important to allow critique in from the outside in order not to lapse into that fantasy. What would be the point of writing, if not to communicate, which sometimes requires more explanation than one would desire."

Magdalena teaches creative writing and martial arts. She leads writing groups at a maximum security prison and in comfortable homes. She was just asked to start one at a woman's prison. During her last stint at the men's prison she got caught up in a riot, but it didn't scare her off. "My theory is that if you choose to write you don't need other, more radical or self destructive, outlets. Writing is healing."

Back then, fifteen years ago, she had one such writing group in Santa Cruz that met weekly. Connie belonged to that group. Connie, who one day asked her to go for a coffee. "I don't know what's wrong with me," she said. "I can hardly listen when you explain something. I keep looking at your lips – it's so strange, I haven't ever felt like this. I almost think I'd like to kiss you."

The tough Captain shrugged. "There's only one way to find out," she said. And that was that.

Connie is the bravest person I know. I imagine how it would be, at sixty-eight, not to know what desire feels like, what falling in love feels like. How it would be to experience that for the first time and not to know how to classify it. What it would mean to speak, to put into words one doesn't have.

"Are you always this honest?" I asked once.

"Well, you know, life is complicated enough. If people keep saying things other than what they mean, it gets totally impossible."

Fifteen years later they're still together, though Connie threatened to end the relationship after two years. "After seventy such a thing is not done!" To Magdalena's surprise, they faced no criticism. For Connie's adult children it was problematic at first that Magdalena was white. And so much younger. The fact that she was a woman bothered no one.

Almost irritated, Magdalena reports of their first trip together. "No one even blinked when we asked for a double room. They thought we were just friends, probably. What is this? Do people think we don't have sex? Just because we have gray hair?" The discrimination she came to expect, didn't hit her anymore.

Magdalena's RV fits snugly into the parking spot in front of my tiny house in Santa Fe. Like my house, the RV is small but has everything one needs, which means less than one thinks. This trimming down is freeing. Especially for someone who lived on a boat for years like Magdalena. After all those years together, she still hasn't moved into Connie's "big house" but instead lives in two sheds in the garden. One is for writing, one for sleeping. Shortly before I returned to Switzerland from San Francisco she let me stay over one night in her shed. A bunk bed, a few books, a light for reading. A knife lodged within reach for protection, even though the area is very safe. At night I heard animals rustling in the garden. I felt like a pirate. I felt free. And untouchable. When you have nothing, you lose nothing.

Compared to Magdalena's shed, my casita feels like a mansion. Especially if you add the patio seating that, in the summer months, serves as my second living room. In the morning when I get up, Magdalena is already sitting there writing, waiting. She closes her computer. "And now? What do you want to do? What have you not yet discovered?"

I hadn't thought about that. I usually move in concentric circles: from the window seat into the garden, from the casita into the neighborhood, down the street and across. From there into the center of town, to the yoga studio and to one of my favorite cafes, one of which is also my favorite book store. Should I ever publish a book in English, Jim from Garcia Street

Books has already offered to organize a book signing. There are points of interest at every corner. What would I like? My time here, that's all. But Magdalena is waiting for an answer.

"The Opera!" I remember. When I was here last time, in my expensive hotel room, I made reservations for tickets for August 1st, Switzerland's National Day. I couldn't have known Magdalena would be here that very day. But it fit. The year before we had celebrated First of August together and far from the old country.

The opera in Santa Fe is mainly famous for not having any walls. The roof, suspended from pillars with cables, was only built after a fire destroyed the original open air theater ten years after its opening in 1957. From the distance it looks like the wings of a giant bird in the red rocks outside the town. Opera season happens to be at the same time as, what here is called monsoon season, and elsewhere summer. Every evening there's a thunderstorm. Often there is a torrential downpour. It mostly stops after twenty minutes but it can last hours. All that is considered in planning the productions and makes for a particular charm. The landscape, nature and weather all challenge the set designers, the light and sound technicians, as well as the singers who often have to compete with rolling thunder.

Magdalena already learned that the tailgate picnic is almost more important than the opera itself. This tradition is derived more from sporting events – the audience shows up hours ahead of the game, unpack their folding tables and mini-grills and fry hamburgers in the parking lot. Presumably the opera audience has more elevated taste. "OK, you got the tickets, I'll deal with the picnic!" Magdalena gets the folding bike from the van and peddles off to Kaune's Market, a neighborhood grocery for the rich and beautiful. She brings back wine, French bread, cheese and pâté, all the wonderful things most health-conscious women our age no longer eat. We get dolled up and drive out to the opera which is located about five miles outside of town. Curtain is scheduled for sunset, at this time of year, around eight thirty. We think we're early but by six thirty the parking lot is nearly full.

No idea what I imagined: an impressionist *dejeuner sur l'herbe*? Wicker baskets and blankets under old shade trees? I know there's no green grass here! And still, I am not prepared for this sight. In the narrow spaces between the tightly parked cars there are folding tables. Some moved their chairs dircctly against the open trunk. The smell of exhaust hangs in the air and it's still hot. At least many of the tables are covered with white linen, with silverware and candle holders. Many couples are dressed up in Victorian costumes, with fancy hats and feather boas. Somebody from the local newspaper is taking pictures, outfits are admired. Umbrellas are ready as well as see-through ponchos and silver thermal blankets of the sort they carry on climbing expeditions.

"We are not prepared," Magdalena decides. We have no tables or chairs, just a blanket that we were going to put down on the nonexistent grass. But the Captain manages to claim a picnic table at the edge of the parking lot. We turn our backs on the SUVs, the paparazzi, the exhaust and enjoy the long distance view into the faraway hills. Magdalena unpacks our picnic. We have a tablecloth, cloth napkins and real glasses. Magdalena opens the wine and hands me the cork.

"Here's to your house purchase," she says.

I look at the cork. "Plan some spontaneity," it says.

In Good Hands

It doesn't take long for my days to acquire a simple definite rhythm. Mornings I go to yoga. I found a studio where I learn something new, a different form of yoga than I'm used to: slower and more precise. And I'm no longer the oldest person in the room. Every time I meet fascinating women, many over seventy, some white-haired, some with wildly hennaed hair or dark blue streaks. Many are dressed creatively in neon colored tiger leotards and most of them are in great shape. A comparatively quietly-dressed beautiful woman, who lies on the yoga mat next to mine, has just finished folding her left shin in front of her face while the right leg lies completely straight on the floor. All that while chatting with her neighbor on the other side as if it were nothing special. She's just warming up. I can only stare. And suddenly I remember seeing that once before, that effortless split.

That was nineteen years ago. After the birth of Cyril I was, kind of, out of shape. I gained forty pounds, as I had done during my first pregnancy. But I was no longer twenty-four, I was thirty-one which was then considered a late pregnancy. My body no longer adjusted as quickly. So I – an avowed couch potato and proud of it – thought I might have to start doing something about my figure. Yoga sounded good, somehow challenging but not too much. The great western yoga mania had not yet hit Switzerland. So I got a video cassette from somewhere (those still existed back then!) and it showed Ali McGraw, the unforgettable beauty from Love Story, executing seemingly impossible contortions in a tight white leotard amid snow white sand dunes, while master teacher Erich Schiffmann gave nasally instructions from off camera. Even now I hear his voice, comforting, when I do the tree pose which requires standing on one leg. "It's OK to sway. Trees sway in the wind."

This video soothed me. I loved it and kept watching it. But still I couldn't force myself to get off the couch and participate. The flow of those moves didn't seem made for the human body – at least not mine.

I stare at the woman next to me. Is it...? Could it be? Maybe the white dunes from the video were in the White Sands National Monument in New Mexico? Didn't Bette Midler, in the role of Sue Menken, talk about how happy Ali McGraw is in Santa Fe? Didn't Armistead Maupin, in one of the interviews about his new residence, tell how you could run into Ali McGraw at the post office?

For the whole hour I have a hard time keeping my drishti, my eye focus. I keep sneaking glances at my neighbor. A bit older, a bit gray along the temples, but still the straight nose, the dense brows. It's her.

After class she sits in the changing room and chats easily with everyone. I dare to speak to her. I tell her the story of the confinement and the video. "Who'd have thought twenty years later I would land in the same yoga class as you!"

She laughs. "That's life – constantly surprising, isn't it?"

"I still have Schiffman's voice in my ear," I say. "Trees..."

"...sway in the wind!" she finishes. And gives me a hug. "Welcome to Santa Fe."

The next week she doesn't remember me, but that no longer matters.

Before my departure I meet with Doris once more. Doris originally came from a village near Bern but she's lived here for more than twenty years. Here she raised her son and kept herself afloat on her own. When I'm with her I feel as though I were accompanying a celebrity. She's known everywhere and gets hailed by all and always has an accompanying story. "She always gave me a great big tip when I worked at the cafe... Our children played together... He used to have four ponies and two mules I looked after for a summer... This used to be the most sought after framemaker in town, my clients stand in line..."

Doris takes care of empty homes when the owners are out of town. She has extraordinary insight into the lives of the rich and famous. Some clients pay her to open their mail or to organize mountains of unused clothing in their closets. In previous years she also used to clean and she can't quite shed her inner Swiss. In our local cafe, a hipster joint called Better Days, she pulls a bottle of Murphy's Oil from her purse, sprays the dingy benches and wipes them clean. "Doesn't that look so much better?" as she smiles at the bearded barista. He can't help but nod. "Doris, you're incredible!" She shrugs. This is completely normal for her. She has the gift of making connections, or rather, unearthing them. At one friend's house she notices the beautiful door knobs, at another's the richly blossoming wisteria. She always asks "Who made these? Where did you find them?" She sees everything, remembers it all. If someone tells her he's bought an old motorcycle. Doris will remember the man who just set himself up as a motorcycle mechanic. Her garden is her own work of art, a rampantly lush but precisely planned oasis. "When I first moved in," Doris said, "there was nothing here. The previous tenants kept mules in the garden shed." By now she can almost provide for herself. In the future she wants to rent out the house and live in the garden shed. It's maybe half the size of my casita. But it holds all she needs. And is surrounded by blossoming bushes where hummingbirds feed outside the window. Here they are again, the tiny houses. Doris shares my fascination. She sends me links to Internet sites, films, forums. There is a whole movement I knew nothing about, the crusade toward small houses. The love of minimal space is mostly borne from necessity but from this necessity grows a need. A need for less rather than more. Reduction instead of expansion. Small rooms force simplicity. They don't allow waste, no chaos, no junk. This constraint relaxes the mind. Once you've lived small you can't go back. I think of Magdalena and her ship cabin reproduction. And how well I slept there.

Could I give it all up and live only in the casita? I don't have to face that question yet. Cyril is still in school. I have my lovely apartment in Aarau, my refuge, and the writing studio where I teach my courses. I have my work that keeps me alive; I have seven pairs of cowboy boots and hundreds of books.

"Would you look after my house as well?" I ask Doris. I know that the houses she's normally in charge of are bigger. Pay better. Besides, she said she wants to work less. But one can always ask.

"Of course," she says.

Everything I tried for years in San Francisco without success suddenly comes easy here in Santa Fe. I have a fully furnished house and someone to look after it. In contrast to the San Francisco house the casita cannot be seen from the road or a parking lot. Thus it can stay empty without being broken into immediately. In time I'm sure I'll be able to rent it out when I am not here. The production companies that film movies and TV series in the area are always looking for temporary lodging, not just villas for their stars but also more modest accommodations for their techs and assistants. So I will be able to travel back and forth depending on my schedule. And stay for longer, a month or more. Cyril lives half with me and half with his father and finds it easier to remain in one place for a longer period of time. Slowly a plan for the future will develop. Even though I know that plans seldom become reality it is nice to realize: It could work like this. I could live this way.

I give Doris the key. She frowns as she reads the fob, "'I got ruined in New Mexico?' – Well, let's hope not."

On my last day here I run into Frederic at the Teahouse. I am leaving as he comes in. He takes a step back when he sees me, almost as if he were afraid of me. He looks like he'd love to turn around. But there's only one entrance. Visibly he catches himself and pastes on a wide smile. "Milena, I can't believe it! How are you, how's the house – you're looking wonderful!"

I smile noncommittally. "Good. Thanks."

He hesitates then pulls himself together. "You got time for a coffee?"

I was about to leave. But I say yes. We look for a table under the trees, study the menu. A tense silence spreads. The more time passes the harder it is to say anything.

What happened to the 'wonderful friendship' I was so sure of? What was it I used to feel? Whatever it was, it's not here anymore. Maybe it never was.

I wait. I say nothing. Not: Where have you been all this time? Not: What kind of behavior is that, just disappearing? Not even: What was all that boasting about the money? That was pretty embarrassing.

I simply wait. Frederic orders. He's nervous.

Our drinks arrive. I stir my iced tea even though I haven't added any sugar.

Finally Frederic says, "We had something, didn't we?" I look up, "Did we?"

"Yes, we shared a piece of the road, a joint task – I was to sell the house, you to buy it."

"That's exactly how I see it," I say. I take another drink from my iced tea, look at my watch. "Got to go," I say. "It was nice seeing you. Thank you for my house."

And then I get up. I leave the iced tea and I leave Frederic to pay the bill. I don't know when I last did something like that. If ever. It was only $2.75, but still, it feels pretty good.

PART III:

HAPPINESS CHALLENGED

Lake Milena Rerun

September 4th, two weeks after my return, my book *Das wahre Leben* comes out. After the opening day launch party I stay over in Zurich with my friend Pie. We talk late into the night, until the "performer's high" dissipates. The next morning I check my mail still half asleep. As though I could spark the high again –someone must have written, reacted, congratulated? The publishing of a book is always connected to a certain emptiness. The moment you've long been waiting for evaporates, explodes. The book is out, the world turns. And my cell phone showed, instead of congratulations, four increasingly urgent messages from Doris: "Call me!"

I call immediately. "What happened?"

"Are you sitting down?" she asks. "No? Then you better do so."

When she went to check on the house for the first time she noticed a puddle at the entrance. She swept it away. A week later she returned and the puddle looked bigger. Doris called a friendly handyman who sent over a couple of guys. They lifted up some floor tiles and discovered a lake under my house. There was water where the crawl space was supposed to be. Two meters deep. The pipes had to have been leaking for months, if not years. Tree roots tunneled through and broke them at certain spots. For months, if not years, the precious water, so strictly rationed in this desert climate, had been seeping into the ground and transforming it into a lake.

I sit. Lake Milena. Just like my dream.

It's late afternoon in Santa Fe. I give Doris the number of Marcia, the manager. "I can't deal with this now," she bellows into the phone at Doris. "I just took a sleeping pill."

"Do what you have to," I tell Doris and she says, "already on it." From five in the morning till eleven at night she's at the house, supervising the work, informing the neighbors – the water for the whole compound has to be turned off. Some of the neighbors react kindly, some irritated. "I need water to wash my hair!" Doris carries buckets of water from across the street. I try to imagine what I'd do without Doris. What would've happened had she not noticed the puddle. The next few days are hectic for me as well. The book tour begins. I have interviews to give and try despite the time difference to be accessible and in the know. It is difficult to deal with this catastrophe by myself. But even more difficult is to talk about it and hear the constant reactions. "Well, that's what you get! Whoever thought of buying a house without thinking? Now you're going to lose it all, the cost of the repairs will ruin you!"

There's a Swiss saying, "You only have yourself to blame if it's your fault." I always liked it for its little twist and now it seems particularly appropriate. Only Pie supports me. She alone remains relaxed. "Old houses need attention," she says. "Old houses cost money. That's just the way it is." So, it's not my fault. Not my failure.

At least I have insurance. It's included as part of the annual dues of the homeowners association. Just to be sure I re-read the contract. Without knowing if the insurance will indeed pay, I give Doris the go-ahead to hire someone to re-lay the pipes. What else could I do? Start a hydroponic farm?

My friends rant. "You've been tricked. That's terrible. How could that happen?"

Yes, how? I think of Marco, the overweight inspector who couldn't get into the crawl space. When he shined the flashlight he would've had to notice the lake, wouldn't he? I think of George who met with the inspector before the arranged time. And, mostly, I think of Frederic. Of how nervous he was when I met him that last time at the Teahouse. Of his almost guilty behavior. I thought he was ashamed for having stopped all contact as soon as he had his money, but now I wonder if there was more.

As it turns out the insurance I pay with my dues only covers the common area. For my unit, my small house, I have to have additional insurance. Everybody does. Everybody knows that. I didn't. How could I have known? Insurance is insurance. I pass on the letter from the homeowners association to George. He reacts right away, appears helpful, reads the hundred pages of terms and conditions and thinks I might have a chance. Because in the terms of the contract my unit is defined by walls, floor and ceiling. The pipes, however, are located outside those boundaries, under the floorboards. Therefore the insurance for the co-op should be responsible for the costs. He even formulates my counter claim. But, like Doris, he doesn't think it's worth involving a lawyer. Lawyers cost a lot of money. Do I really want to introduce myself to my neighbors by suing them?

While I wait for an answer from the insurance, Jean-Francois and his men continue work under Doris's supervision. She sends pictures. I stare at one for a long time without understanding the blue spot in the middle. Only after a while I recognize the bent back of a man in a blue T-shirt. He's kneeling in a hole in my living room, six feet below the floor boards.

Where once was my living room, now there is water. A lake. It looks exactly like in my dream except that the water isn't blue, but brown. It's incredible that I lived on top of that lake without knowing it. That Frederic lived on the lake without ever knowing?

The whole living room floor has to be raised so the lake can dry out. Only then can the pipes be replaced. At least that shouldn't take very long in the desert climate. Only, in this particular year it rains for the whole month of September. The town hasn't seen such a wet September in a hundred years. The Santa Fe river swells, green grass grows along the levy and my living room has a high tide.

I send Frederic the pictures without comment. Against all expectations he responds immediately. "OMG! I'm afraid to ask...!" I explain the situation without accusation. He shows himself properly shocked and suggests I should contact the owner of the gallery in the front house – they had the same problem the year before and the insurance paid.

The homeowner's association refuses all liability. After the water damage in the gallery had been discovered, all the common water lines from the street to the compound were replaced at the expense of the communal insurance. The pipes leading from the communal space to the individual units were supposed to be replaced by each owner at his own cost, or covered by his private insurance. To keep the cost down, nearly everybody decided to have the work done simultaneously and by the same firm. I receive a copy of the minutes of last year's meeting when this decision was made. The minutes were signed by Frederic as well. He was even a member of the board that made those decisions.

Shortly after this meeting he must have decided to sell his house. Because he didn't have the money for new pipes. Do I? I still don't know what the whole thing will cost. Jean-Francois can't give a quote as long as everything is under water.

"At least sixty thousand," Katchie guesses.

"Sixty thousand?" That would be the end. It would break me.

Katchie is upset with me. "You should never have depended on Frederic's real estate agent, you should've worked with Lisa, she would never have let you accept this so-called inspection."

"I know, I know! But that doesn't exactly help me now!" I snap back.

The only one keeping her cool is Pie. "Will it ruin you to fix the problem?"

I shrug. "I don't have any money left, if that's what you mean."

"Can you afford it?"

"I don't know. I don't even know how much it will be."

"There are really only two possibilities," Pie says. "Either you can pay for the new pipes without ruining yourself and you'll pull it off. Or you won't. Then you'll have to sell the house or take out another loan. Pipes break, that's a fact of life. Roofs, too. There will always be something. An old house is like an old dog. You love it, you take care of it." I hold on to that until Jean-Francois finally emails me a quote: ten thousand dollars. Much less than I feared. I can just do it. And am back at the original sale price.

My friends demand revenge. Frederic should pay. Frederic should be punished! The fact he cheated me is one thing but that he flirted with me to get what he wanted is another. They are outraged on my behalf or in my name. Because, strangely enough, I don't feel anything. Yes, I could sue him. He, at the very least, falsified a certified statement claiming he was not aware of any major damages to the house. The minutes of the meeting a year ago prove that this is untrue. He lied. So, yes, I have a case – and then? I know he has no money. And I've already struggled with one court case in a country where I don't understand the laws. So I decide to let it go. And I do. Let it go.

Why am I not upset? Is that a weakness, foolishness? Or wisdom? I think less often of Frederic's behavior than of the outcome. What if I had I forced the inspector to check the crawl space? What if I had known that all the pipes had to be replaced? My conviction that I was right in buying this house would have been shaken. I believe in signs. Maybe I would have even stepped back from the purchase. If not, I would've immediately started the repairs and would have spent the remaining summer with bids and workers and ever new catastrophes. I couldn't have lived in the house. I wouldn't have had those weeks with Cyril, with Magdalena.

"At least you would've saved money," Katchie insists.

She's right. I call it learning money. If I'm honest, I have already paid out lots, maybe too much. "OK, you're right," I say. "In the future I'll be more careful."

And in the past? What, I wonder, if I was able to see the ending of my marriage the same way? Looking at it from the end, the result? What if I transferred some of the serenity, the generosity I feel for Frederic, onto my ex husband? For two years I've obsessed over his behavior. I still don't understand it, I can't get past it. But what if I looked at the end result?

I am free. Maybe it was the only way I could free myself from this connection that was as unhappy as it seemed destined and unbreakable. He did the one thing I could not forgive, the one thing that bars all return. He made me think I was crazy. But this unforgivable act freed me. For the first time I can feel the possibility of being grateful to him. If I can be grateful to Frederic, why not him too?

Throwing Bricks

Six weeks after my return to Switzerland I am lying on a cot in the ER in the Kanton's hospital in Aarau and waiting to be inserted into a tube. "We don't know what's wrong," the neurologist said. "Probably nothing. But I would prefer to be sure. After all you'll be needing your brain."

Will I? How the hell did I get here?

I had hardly slept for several nights. Two days before I had locked myself out of my apartment. I was out to dinner with Sibylle, drank a bit too much but on the way home sobered up. Like so many times before I missed the train by mere minutes, then drank some coffee at the station. I used to get irritated by such things. When we first arrived back in Switzerland I lived according to the train schedule, knew exactly when my trains were coming and constantly checked my watch. I no longer do that. I go to the station when the evening is over and I either catch a train or I wait. It was nearly midnight when I stood outside my apartment in the rain. I dug through my purse, no keys, but I know that one. Come on, I think as so often before of a kind of informal prayer, come on, don't do that. Not now. I sit down on a bench, turn over my whole purse – no keys. It's nearly midnight. Cyril is in Poland with his school. For a moment I consider calling Sara who lives near the train station but she always has to get up extra early, plus she is in the middle of sesshin, the intensive meditation training week. So I go to the hotel at the station but they don't have any rooms. The nearest hotel with a night clerk is in Lenzburg, the next small town, about 10 miles away. How will I get there at this time of night? The receptionist looks up the number of a locksmith, I call, they won't come. It would take too long, it would cost too much, it would be better to stay in a hotel. Maybe I should go back to Zurich? In the meantime the last train is gone. For a wild instant I consider sleeping outside, on a park bench, the night is mild despite the rain. Back at the hotel, the receptionist calls Lenzburg. I am desperate, in tears, but I don't think anything of being seen that way by this man. I take the taxi to Lenzburg, sixty francs. I get the last room, one hundred and ten francs. A very nice woman supplies me with a toothbrush. She recognizes me, "You're Milena Moser? I always read your columns."

"Yes," I say. "You see? This is my life! I'm not fabricating anything!"

The next morning I have an appointment at the American embassy in Bern. I want to renew my visa. The next step on my way back to America. The paperwork is in my apartment. There is still a chance I didn't lose the keys but locked them inside the apartment. If I can get in the main entrance I still might make the appointment. But the shoe store on the ground floor only opens at nine, while my train leaves at eight. I sleep for a few hours, wake up at five and suddenly remember: Trudy has a key! My cleaning lady. She lives very close to Lenzburg. I get up, get dressed and wait till six before I call. I wake her – very unusual, she says, she normally gets up early. She brings me the key, drives me to the Lenzburg train station, I catch the next train to Aarau, sprint home. I open the main entrance with my key, climb up the stairs - my apartment door is unlocked! I never locked it, the keys are in the bowl by the entrance where they always are. I grab the file folder, hurry back to the station and catch the train to Bern. I'm on time for my appointment, I get my visa. And I'm completely exhausted. That night I hardly sleep either. On Thursday I have signed up for a zazenkai with Sara. A day long program, some meditation, some conversation, a bit of gardening from six in the morning till five in the afternoon. Afterward I plan to meet Nicki and go to the museum with her. That morning I also take advantage of the opportunity for daisan, a personal conversation with the teacher. I tell Sara the whole key story. "You always go the most difficult route," she says. Then she gets irritated and wants to know why I didn't ring her doorbell.

"I thought you… you always have to get up so early and your place is so small…"

"So? I have a whole yoga studio full of mats and blankets," she says. And, "if you don't ever challenge a relationship there will always be a certain distance."

I think about that: the distance. The fathomless despair I felt when I was wandering around the old city in the middle of the night. I am all alone, nobody helps me, I have nobody. When, in fact, all I had to do was ring a doorbell. That I also had a neighbor who could have let me into the house only occurs to me now, two days later. She was probably even still awake. I have to learn to ask for help if I want to find out if anyone will ever be there for me. It doesn't happen by itself.

The weather is beautiful. Ruth comes as well, now we're three and I enjoy working in the garden. I am relegated to pulling weeds which I like as I can day-dream. In the meantime Sara turns over a mound of earth. Suddenly she stops and says "you hear something?" I stand up. For a moment everything turns black and I grab hold of a post. It passes. From the mound a tiny high squeak erupts. A mouse nest? Sara turns white. "I almost stuck the shovel into the mice!" she says. A mouse slaughter – a terrible thought. I kneel down again, I'm dizzy. Sara notices and sends me over to the rose hedge, so I can work standing up. I keep getting weaker and more shaky. Finally I lie down on the bench, then in the grass. After an hour I feel it's getting worse and I say I want to go home. I don't want the two women to accompany me; I'm embarrassed because I left my apartment a mess with everything strewn all over, clothes, laundry, dishes. They insist on coming along. Sara wants to stop at the pharmacy to check my blood pressure. I don't want to. "I have an app for that," I say and laugh, feeling a bit tipsy. We walk along the street, I stagger without realizing it. When we get to the crossroads a bus happens to stop. Sara pulls me onto the bus, Ruth jumps in behind. We'll drive to the medical office at the train station, Sara decides. Later she tells me that a year earlier a friend asked if she could teach him a good stretch, he sometimes had these strange pains in his chest and arm after jogging. Two days later he died of a heart attack. She didn't want to repeat that.

To distract me Sara talks at me the whole time we're on the bus. She says the clinic is fine if you don't have a primary care physician, those doctors are happy to have something to do during the week. Only on weekends are they busy with alcohol poisonings and knife wounds. When we get to the station, however, the waiting room is busy. A receptionist comes immediately and says, "She's feeling that bad?" while pointing at me. I am amazed. Do I look it? She sends us on to the acute care department on a higher floor. There I'm put on the cot and receive an infusion. The whole situation seems completely surreal and more and more I have trouble explaining what is going on. But I feel pretty good, actually almost tipsy. It becomes more and more essential that I stress I'm not taking drugs. The more I insist the stranger it appears. Sara keeps trying to point that out to me, but she can't get through. When I need to go to the bathroom, the doctor decides Sara needs to go with me.

"Talk about testing friendship," I say. "About distance."

My lips are numb. "I can't talk clearly anymore," I tell Sara, but the doctor overhears and decides to transfer me to the Kantonsspital. In an ambulance. Now I'm getting worried. I cry

"I don't want to go to the hospital." Ruth decides she'll return to the Zendo and inform Eric, Sara's husband. Later she'll tell us that she lay down on the meditation mats and slept for two hours. The EMTs use the English words "possible stroke victim" on their radio.

"I understand English," I want to say, "I know what stroke means." The EMT questions me and I can tell he too finds my story suspicious. "What kind of meditation do you practice?" he asks. "And what do you grow in that garden?" Somehow I thought Zen was a known term, a seal of quality almost, and I just meant to stress how quiet, how calm, the morning had been.

"This practice is not for the faint of heart," our Roshi once said. And I, as if shot from a cannon, said, "I am not!" It came out loud and convincing. "I am not faint of heart!" But now, yes. I am exactly that. I feel weaker and weaker, as if my bones and muscles have dissolved and my skin is filled with raw cotton. Or with white smoke. I'm trying to describe the symptoms to one doctor after another. Sara later says she wouldn't be surprised if her Zen center got shut down – what I put on here was not very good publicity. But she remains by my side, mediating. "No, I know her, she doesn't usually speak so slowly. No, normally what she says makes sense."

"Are you scared?" the chief neurologist asks.

"No." Again I try to describe how I feel and keep coming back to the drug comparison. Sara confirms, "It's as though she were poisoned." I was babbling, Sara later says. Most of it incomprehensible. I am unaware. I only know that I'm slow, that I float, that I am out of control. The doctor listens to my explanations with a frown.

"If you keep looking at me like this I *will* get scared," I say.

"That's the first normal reaction you've shown!" Then she asks about the plants, the garden, checks my hands for cuts through which something – what? – could've entered my system.

I have to use the bathroom again; the doctor says I should get up to show her that I can stand. I steady myself with my calves against the bed frame, she notices. "Take one step forward. Stand on one leg." It's not working. The aid brings the potty chair and consoles me that at least it's not the bed pan. Later the report reads that I was communicating and moving normally the whole time.

The chief orders an MRI. Just to be safe. The technician cuts off all my lucky charms from my wrists. They give me ear plugs because it's loud inside the machine. For one moment I'm filled with superstitious fear. I have written about brain tumors and multiple sclerosis. Maybe that is my punishment? Doesn't MS start with vertigo? Despite the hammering inside and despite my fear I almost fall asleep, strangely removed. I don't hear the technicians who announce the end of the examination. The aide who comes to get me notices the missing charm bracelets and is irritated because all afternoon he took such great care not to cut them off while placing the IV needle or taking my blood pressure.

In the mean time Eric has arrived. He brings sandwiches and chocolate bars for everyone. Immediately I feel better. I desperately want to leave. I want to go home.

"You're suddenly speaking better," Sara says. And to the aide, "she's herself again." I'm glad there's someone here who knows me. Who knows how I am. Now I'm impatient. The discharge papers take forever. I keep stepping out into the hallway, maybe just to prove how well I can walk. At one of the excursions in search of the neurologist in charge I run into the EMT who drove me here.

"And?" he asks. "Did they find anything?"

"No."

Again he asks if maybe this meditation could've caused something to break loose and again I say, "No, we just sit there and breathe." I can hear how strange that sounds. I can see he thinks I'm crazy, the kind of woman who has only herself to blame. Finally we all move to the waiting room because I can't stand the hospital room any longer. I thank my aide for all his help and add, "I hope I never see you again!" He answers, "Who knows, Aarau is a small town after all."

Finally the intern comes in and discharges me. Without results. He says sometimes there are physical reactions more subtle than those medical school can cover. That sounds a bit better than "You're probably crazy." And he wishes me luck.

I still feel a bit shaky and hollow. And vaguely guilty. What a drama! What a lot of effort! For what? Nothing.

The three of us walk back to town. Shortly before the train station a bicycle rider passes us. "What did I tell you? Aarau is tiny." The rider calls out. It's the nurse's aide from before.

In the old town there is a fair; it is crowded with people, food booths, smells, and right away a wave of dizziness hits me. We buy some Thai food on the corner and Sara and Eric walk me all the way to my door. I startle when I see the blue trash bags set out on my street.

"What's the matter?"

"I forgot to take the trash out of the studio."

I want to turn back and take care of it but Sara and Eric dissuade me. They find it ridiculous but it bothers me. I need to have things done, the laundry folded, the dishwasher emptied, the trash taken out for pickup. I can't relax until everything is done. I am aware that this behavior is irrational but it doesn't help. And so I wait in the entrance until they have disappeared around the corner. I sneak back into my writing studio and set the bags of trash out. Only then can I relax. I go back up to my apartment where I lie down on the sofa, eat my curry directly from the carton, watch TV, make phone calls.

I cancel two personal dates. Not professional ones. How could I? With what explanation? I had a – what? – pseudo stroke? My body produces arbitrary drugs that put me out of commission for hours? Because I am crazy after all?

Is it now proven? The struggle I fought during recent years, all the hours of therapy, of talks, disputes. Just to learn to trust my intuition, to listen to my inner voice. To prove that I'm not crazy. To prove it, primarily to myself. I can now give up the fight.

During the past years I had a lot of interactions with burned out patients who somehow ended up in my writing studio. Repeatedly I wondered if the exhaustion I was feeling was something similar. But I love my work! It's the only stability I know. When I heard about a stay-at-home mom who was clinically burned out I thought for the first time: maybe artists burn out as well. "My body told me things couldn't go on this way," I kept hearing. My body quit. But my body is as healthy as a horse. What the hell does it want to tell me with this episode?

And then I remember something the American talk show host Oprah Winfrey, who sees herself as a spiritual guide, often says, "God tickles you first with a feather but if you don't react, sooner or later She'll have to resort to bricks." Was this one of those bricks? But why a brick made of cotton? Of air? An imaginary brick?

I distract myself with TV watching a few hours of the American family saga *Parenthood*. It's the only series where I don't skip the opening credits because I love the theme song, Bob Dylan's "Forever Young." That song makes me over-sentimental, makes me think of my sons – and of myself.

"May you always do for others, and may others do for you..."

The line makes me tear up every time. That others might do something for me!

Only, this time I listen closely. It doesn't say "may others do for you" but "*let* others do for you."

Traveling (Book-) Saleswoman

On the train in Northern Germany, between Hamburg and Nordhorn, between Nordhorn and Leer. An empty landscape passes outside the window, windblown birch trees in fall colors that bring to mind the song by Hildegard Knef as sung by Michael Von der Heide: "I need a change of wallpaper said the birch..." Me too, I think. I look out the window, outside it's flat.

I think back to all the book tours I have done. To my first visit to the book fair as an author rather than a bookstore apprentice. How nervous I was, how impressed. How I automatically got coffee for the others. At the booth of my first "real" publishing house the hierarchy was subtly but clearly demarcated by a red sofa. Not all the authors were allowed to sit there. I only made it once – when I was very pregnant. "I wanted a book of yours, not a baby," the editor said. And I, "the baby you won't get! But the book, yes." I have never yet not delivered. No matter the circumstances... but is this really a virtue? I'm beginning to doubt.

On my early book tours I usually stayed at the booksellers' homes. Later I was flown in business class and put up in first class hotels, sometimes even accompanied every step by an assistant.

I remember how homesick I was. When one time I saw a train destined for Zurich, my then hometown, and had to force myself not to jump on it, but instead continue traveling. To the next town, the next reading. How long did those trips take? I don't remember. A week, ten days? Two weeks with a free weekend? At some point I had early contractions and the doctor suggested I cancel a few appearances. Which I did, though the organizers were rather irritated. For the baby I could do it. But not for myself.

Suddenly all the book fairs mix up in my mind, all the readings. Huge halls, tiny spaces, empty chairs, too few chairs... days at the book fair when one appointment chases the next and I don't get a chance to sit down, let alone eat. Others, when I stand around and am mistaken for a staff member of the publisher's. I don't mind. "You're not a regular author," I keep hearing. "You're one of us. Could you look after author so and so, I think he's sulky because..." I used to take it as a compliment: You're too nice to be a regular author.

There were glamorous moments – and some that were less than so. A TV crew followed me on my first reading tour to Germany. But already the first stop turned out to be a misunderstanding. The book store that invited me sells only political mysteries. And however much you tried – there was no political message in my early mysteries. The already scarce audience was irritated. The cameraman turned to the director, "Should we make a loser story of it?"

A suite in the Frankfurter Hof. I order High Tea that comes on a rolling table. On a pyramid finger sandwiches and scones are piled high, enough for me and prince Charles plus the two favorite dogs of the Queen of England. The room service waiter pours the tea, then turns chalk white. With a gloved finger he points to the bathroom door under which foam bubbles out. I forgot I was going to take a bath.

An hour of signing books was marked on my program but the organizer had forgotten. When I showed up someone quickly scribbled my name on a piece of paper with a marker and set my chair next to a very famous and well-publicized fantasy author. The line of his fans went around the block. Since no one wanted anything from me I started tearing the protective covers from his books, efficiently, the way I had learned to do during my apprenticeship as a young girl. Once learned, never forgotten.

Full houses, empty houses, six lost souls dropped among fifty chairs, somewhere in the Ruhr, I can't remember where. "Would you mind moving closer?" I begged. And the six people who had never met before, moved so close together that they all took me out to dinner afterwards.

Last shouts in hotel bars. Drunk authors. Somewhere the last facade crumbles.

"Tell me, how old are you?"

"Fifty."

"Really? You don't look a day over forty-four, I swear. Should we go to my room?"

I laugh. "I would need a little more than that," I say.

"Oh, no problem, I have some drugs in my room!" I take my half-empty glass up to my room, alone. Still laughing. But also a little tired of it all. Been there, done that. I keep thinking that more and more often.

I look out the window over the flat land that to me seems gray. Maybe that, too, is the price of exhaustion: not to see color in the world. I remember a Swiss couple I met the day before at a reading; they sat with us afterwards. They had been living on a boat for five years and lay at anchor outside of Leer. She wore a handmade sweater that went well with her flame colored hair. They told, obviously not for the first time, how they had come to leave their old lives behind. Just as interesting were the questions we asked them. I wanted to know first off how old their children were, twenty and twenty-two. More or less as mine would be next year. If I left then? Rieke wanted to know how it was with relationships, friends, the feeling of connection with a community. And Antje, whether a new place ever felt like home. "And what about your stuff?" I continued. " Don't you miss your things?" All those things that accumulate in a life. And don't fit on the boat. Or in a house of 550 square feet. The questions we ask reveal our own personal preoccupations. Rieke has finished her wandering and now appreciates the ties to her place of birth. And Antje would never want to move away from the only home she knows. And me? The idea of giving up everything, of jettisoning ballast, tempts me. And I wonder how it will be for my children. When I'm so far away. Possibly they'll be relieved?

I turn the ring on my finger, a silver Katchina with a coral in its belly. Katchinas are figures representing dancers that carry certain ghostly powers. A triply encapsulated symbol. The ring seems misplaced here, on this train, in this landscape. I bought it from a Swiss vendor at the flea market in Santa Fe. She told me she had just given up her house in Taos. Not for a smaller apartment, not for a boat, for nothing. She no longer had a permanent residence. The decision didn't seem to have been completely voluntary but she formulated it bravely and very un-Swiss. She didn't complain, she didn't say "I'm homeless." She said she wanted to be independent, to be able to leave any time to visit her son who is married in Switzerland. She just came back from there after taking care of her father until his death. But stay there, no she couldn't do that. Now she's back in New Mexico, selling her jewelry at flea markets, sleeping at friends' and sometimes house sitting. The Katchina ring is not part of her display, she wears it on her middle finger.

"I love this one," I say.

She takes it off and hands it to me. "I've worn it through all the changes of the recent years," she says. "It was a great companion for that. Take it, it suits you."

I turn the ring on my finger and look out at the gray landscape. The ring suits me but does it suit my life? Do I still suit my life?

From the Life of an Insane Woman

At six in the evening I arrive back in Aarau after nearly twelve hours on the train. I'm exhausted and call my son from the train. "I'll pick up some Chinese at the train station. I'm too tired to cook." He's fine with that. Chicken Kung Pao and spring rolls, all very healthy. At home I do three loads of laundry. Actually I was going to iron my long summer dress but I'm too tired.

The next morning a two-day workshop starts. I get up at seven, iron the dress, and try it on in case it no longer fits. The workshop goes until five after which I have half an hour to throw on my "festive evening attire," put on makeup, comb my hair. For weeks I've been thinking about how I would manage that and what I would wear. Pie, the only of my girlfriends who knows about stuff like that, opines "If the invitation says 'festive evening dress' it means you get picked up in a limousine." Not, that you rush in this attire through icy winds and ugly weather dragging your dress through icy slush and dirty snow. That, by the way, is the origin of the word slut. Initially it used to mean slatternly seams, only later the wearer herself. A good example for the fact that no matter what you do you can't please everybody: a slattern is as much a woman who drags her seams carelessly in the mud, a sloppy, muddled person, as one who raises her dress too high and shows some leg, a woman free with her charm. Of course both are not right – but so much fun!

Fun? Exactly. If an invitation that reads "festive evening attire" causes only stress and no fun, you are definitely doing something wrong.

I know that, and still I can't change it. I race home, change, quickly put on makeup. Pullover over the dress, coat, scarf, thick winter boots. High heels in the purse, along with the invitation. By the time I get to the train station my hair is wet, my mascara is smeared, my nose is running. I take the train to Baden, which takes another half an hour. Then the taxi to the marquee. Some prize I was nominated for but didn't get is being handed out and I'm supposed to be present, so it said in the contract. I missed the walk down the red carpet and the seats at the table have been allocated to someone else. We look at each other, I and my friend Nikolaus who kindly agreed to be my escort. We might as well leave, we are both thinking. We haven't seen each other for a long time. Why don't we go to a Pizzeria or his or my place? But the chairs are being moved, the empty plates cleared away. Wine is being poured. We try to talk across the table during the small breaks. Nikolaus doesn't show it, but in his eyes I mirror my own unease. What the hell are we doing here? Good question.

What the hell am I doing here?

The week before I had watched a German documentary about John Irving, "The World according to John Irving." Pie handed me the DVD with the words "that's how I imagine your next husband." And, indeed, I fell in love immediately. An old man with a jump rope! Hands in pizza dough. Fantastic. But men like this, the film makes abundantly clear, need strong women. And so I concentrate on the essential, the writing.

The film portrait starts with the author sweating on a mat doing core exercises, weights. In the background young wrestlers in unflattering outfits practice the same holds over and over. Again and again and again. Years of hard training taught him, so says Irving, the mixture of dedication and discipline necessary for an author of long novels that require much re-writing. "The process of writing resembles athletic training. No one watches, no one applauds, there is no winning or losing. Only repetition. A kind of drill. And that's how you spend most of your life, whether you're an artist or an athlete." And before you can assume that the book tour shown in the film, the nine hundred spectators, the film cameras, the applause are the reward for years of dedication and discipline, Irving makes it clear: It's the exact opposite. The appearance in public is the price he pays for long undisturbed months at his desk. "I do that for my publisher. It buys me another five or six years at the desk."

He finds the reward at the desk, in solitude, in the repetition. "The idea that repetition – to keep doing something over and over – should not be boring but essential..." What happens at a desk, really, is hard to describe and even harder to show in a film. "It occurs so slowly! The audience would fall asleep watching an author write!" I know exactly what he means. This is precisely what I yearn for, this slowness, this undisturbed time of writing.

The next prize winner is being introduced, the plates are removed. There's dessert. "Let's go," I say to Nikokaus. He jumps up right away.

Despite the early departure it is nearly midnight when I finally make it back home. Since we missed half of the dinner, I'm still hungry. Or maybe just unfulfilled. I eat a piece of bread and some cheese, drink a glass of wine while standing. In the dark kitchen window I see a mirrored image of myself. I'm still wearing my coat over the festive attire which, in reality, is a long, flowery summer dress.

I put down the glass and shake my head. "What the hell?" I ask the figure in the glass. "What do you want?"

The answer comes out of nowhere and makes my knees buckle. I don't want to be a writer any longer!

And I never wanted anything else. Even before I knew I wanted to have children I knew that I wanted to be a writer. It is the only certainty I ever held onto. Through all the changes in recent years this was my last hold. And now this hold is letting go. The floor opens beneath me and I fall. I fall into a deep well, I can't catch myself anywhere. For three days I sit in the bottom of this well. It is dark, cold and dank. I am alone. I draw up my knees and wrap my arms around.

What is left? I have no family. I have no husband. My children are nearly grown. I have no home. What remains if I lose my work as well? If I no longer can practice it the way it is demanded these days?

Suddenly I am reminded of my first class reunion, the only one I ever went to. I was very happy to leave childhood and youth as far behind as possible and I looked back as seldom as I could. I think it was fifteen years after primary school, so I must have been about twenty-nine. I had published two or three books and had already been "on TV." Nevertheless I didn't want to go, my memories were too negative. A friend, my only one from back then, said "you've got to! Exorcism and such!"

So I went and it wasn't bad. What had I expected? That they'd show me the door? That they'd laugh at me? At some point I sat at a table with a bunch of women and the conversation turned to "what was her name, the one with the knock knees?"

"... who ran so funny...!"

Whine, snicker, brawl. I grow cold all over. "That was me," I said. Glances roam across the table to me. "What are you talking about, of course, that wasn't you! You were always cool! No, you know, the one with the German father... and the mother who kept showing up at school."

"That was me."

"Now, stop it, not you – it was… what was her name... You all remember she cried at an exam because she had one grade below an A..."

"...because my father had just come from the doctor, he had heart disease." But they didn't believe me. I couldn't be the outsider, they couldn't have ridiculed me. I was, after all. "on TV." I was famous. To be famous redeemed me in the eyes of my former antagonists – but not my own. To be famous hasn't changed anything where it counts, inside.

Instead I reinvented myself. I created a world in which the outsiders run things. There, in my writing, I redeem myself. Writing saves me. Not the having written. Even less the being an author. For others this might be the source of happiness, not for me. Not for John, either.

After three days at the bottom of this well it suddenly gets lighter. Fear gives way to bone-deep relief. What remains when I'm no longer mother, wife, writer? Nothing.

Just me.

It is enough.

I stand and look up. The edge of the well only reaches my hips. I climb out with ease.

The Financial Consultant

My tax accountant sends me to a pension fund adviser. "I would just like to know if you're hedged. For the future." I would like to know that, too. I collect all my papers and take the train to Bern.

I keep remembering the Voodoo priestess Madame Denise who told me my main theme was retreat. That I wanted to retire. Back then I rejected the idea. She's wrong about that, I thought, I'm only just getting started! Now I keep thinking more and more that she was right. I need a *posada*, a place to rest. Is Santa Fe this place? Is Santa Fe the place she meant and couldn't yet name? After all, there are many others who relax there. Who retire there. But how to do it? My plan is to spend six months in Switzerland and earn enough for the whole year. But the mere thought makes me want to lie down and never get back up. I know somehow that I can't do this any longer.

I'm as nervous as a child called to the headmaster's office. I am pretty sure I did everything wrong. But the consultant looks carefully at my paperwork and, to my amazement, states I did everything correctly. I even have loss of earnings insurance! I had completely forgotten about that. Some time over the last several years my therapist said, "In Germany, first off we would send you to a clinic for a three-month course of treatment at a convalescence clinic." And I, "Well, that would be nice but I don't live in Germany." Now I realize that I could've gone on sick leave, prescribed by a doctor! I could've had myself committed to a clinic behind white walls and green hedges, to find myself again and to really recover! How many people, known or overheard, have discussed this very thing and while I envied them for the possibility? And all this time I had the option! Why oh why did I not remember this insurance?

Now I recall how reluctantly I signed those papers. I had to literally be pressured into it. "What is your family supposed to live on if you should break down?"

"I can write in a hospital bed," I said stubbornly.

"Not if it's your head that is affected..."

"OK, fine!"

Signed and forgotten. By the time I needed the insurance, not for the family but for myself, I couldn't remember that I had it.

"Do you see a possibility for me to work less?" I ask.

The consultant looked through my papers again. I have the suspicion he knows the answer already.

"Not a chance," he says quietly. "As long as you keep living in Switzerland you have to continue working the same. You could, of course, get a cheaper apartment, but that doesn't make the roast fat..."

Even though I have all three types of retirement accounts that are mandatory in Switzerland, they didn't grow sufficiently during the short years I was employed. Since I didn't contribute to them when I was self-employed, which was most of my life, there is not enough to sustain me in a hypothetical retirement. The divorce lawyer was already worried about that. "Are you sure you'll manage?" she asked. I was almost offended. "Of course," I said, "I always manage!"

"If you emigrate," the consultant continued "you could of course withdraw everything. But that is also only enough for..." Again he combs through the documents which, by now, he must know by heart, "One year, maybe two." He spreads his arms apologetically. It's not his fault. The decisions I've made in my life have been my very own. Stupid, idealistic, star struck, maybe -- but my own.

I try for flippant, "Who knows, maybe my next book will become a film or be translated and be a bestseller..." Anything is possible, after all.

But the consultant doesn't dwell in possibilities. "Other than that, do you have any investments, shares, real estate?"

"Well, yeah..." Since it can't get any worse now I tell him about my house in San Francisco that, supposedly, is my pension plan but that I do not ever want to sell. "It's the only home my sons still have," I say. "Even if I don't plan to ever live there again. It could change. Besides, it's the only thing I can leave them one day."

If I can even keep it. In a few weeks I fly back to San Francisco to appear before the court. The American legal drama shows that I've been watching religiously since I found out the court date don't exactly encourage me to put my faith in the American legal system. But I don't tell him that. I don't want to hear, yet again and from an authority no less, how I did everything wrong. Only that the original plan that I would return to San Francisco one day has faltered because, for one thing, I can't afford the city any longer. For another, I can't rent out the house furnished and month to month. "Instead I now have a casita in Santa Fe where this is theoretically possible," I say defiantly and wait for his professional scolding. But it doesn't come.

"Hmm. Couldn't you lease out your San Francisco house long-term?"

"Yes, that is possible." In the meantime my lawyer has connected me with an agency that does this. They make up the contract, choose the renters and make sure they leave in time and don't file absurd law-suits. The high cost of living in San Francisco means that the rents are high as well.

"What can you expect, more or less? What kinds of taxes do you pay there, how much does the agency charge?" He puts the numbers into the computer. "And the other house, you say, is in Santa Fe – that is New Mexico, right?" Again he taps something. Obviously there is an Internet site to find the average cost of living in any chosen place in the world.

Now he smiles for the first time. "That's your solution! You can live in Santa Fe off the rent from San Francisco! Voila!"

Voila! Voila? I have a solution? But that's not all.

"And since the house probably won't depreciate, your sons, too, will be provided for one day."

Re-voila! All questions answered, all problems solved, there's nothing more to do. I leave the office in shock. The most absurd, impulsive and irrational decision of my life turns out to be the best. I have saved myself! I can get out! I am free!

I call Pie from the train. Against all expectation she is indignant. "But, if you can live off the rent from San Francisco, why don't you do it? Why hasn't anyone told you this? For years you've been slaving away when you had a way out the whole time?"

"Well, no, not really. It could only work this way now. Only the casita made it possible." The rent wouldn't be enough to live on in Switzerland or San Francisco. But in Santa Fe it is.

Assuming, of course, that I can keep the house in San Francisco. And assuming I give up everything here. The great apartment in Aarau, my beloved writing studio, as well as my plan B, a room in the apartment of a friend in Zurich, a place to come back to and store some of my belongings. And, speaking of belongings, also everything I've accumulated in my apartment and the writing studio.

When I get home I pace off the apartment like a collections official. I take a close look at everything. The furnishings, the pictures, the bookshelves. The row of boots at the entrance, the closets full of clothes, the rugs, the lampshades, the candle holders, the photo albums, the jewelry. The plants on the terrace, the colorful garden chairs – my only designer furniture I brought from the dream house. So many things, so many memories, so many lives, so much living.

There is the heavy cherry wood secretary desk I inherited from my grandfather. He died when I was nine years old. The valuable piece has seen much and suffered much. As a child I used to do craft projects on it, and it was soon spattered with clay and spotted with paint. The massive desk was the nightmare of all movers. Before I could afford professionals, my friends used to ask, "does the THING come too? Because if so, I have plans for Saturday..."

I lost the key for the secret drawer early on. For years I imagined what, as a child, I might have hidden there. A diary? Stolen sweets? At move number something, a friend opened the drawer with a paper clip and brought out, to the amusement of others and the embarrassment of myself, a photo of Bernhard Russi, Swiss Ski Champion of the Seventies, son-in-law of the Nation, complete with doodles of hearts and flowers.

In every shared apartment, in every dream house on every continent, wherever I lived, the bureau stood. In the casita there's no room for it. Nor for the beautiful antique country armoire that used to be in my mom's childhood bedroom and then, for years, at my brother's house. And now in my apartment, in the old town with its uneven floors, it leans like a tired old man against the wall. I can't bring myself to tell it, "Sorry but your journey has not yet ended, you'll have to get up again, move once more."

I won't be able to bring anything other than some clothes, boots, books. The books! As an author and life-long book nerd I have never managed to throw out a book. Even if I'll never read it again. Like the Russian classics in the cheap East German editions that, back then, I could order dirt cheap through the bookstore where I did my training. They probably have historical value by now!

And the pieces left over from my father's French library, though, as far as I know he couldn't read French. Uncut pages in yellowed paper, some already disintegrating. First editions from the sixties, never read. Since then my French has worsened to the point I probably won't read them either. For close to ten years a box has been sitting in the basement with the complete collection of American women's mystery writers published for the first time in German. Those I read, every one, whether I liked them or not. I was so happy they existed. Presumably they have collector's value. If they're not completely moldy.

The self-help gurus who tell my life story as a series of crises: *M.o.M Mother Without Man. Mama's Newest Boyfriend. War Zone Patchwork Family. Every Child Can Sleep. What's Wrong With Mama? Fail With Ease. With the Next Man Everything Will Be Different.* What do I really need? What does everything really mean? Which memories are intractably connected with things, which ones can I dislodge and carry in my heart? Those are the kinds of considerations I recognize from my mother who moved from a big house into a small apartment that used to belong to a friend who had moved into an assisted living facility.

From them both I inherited things for which they no longer had space, dishes, books, pieces of furniture. Also from strangers. In my writing studio there is a handmade wall hanging with colored pockets full of post cards from the seventies and eighties. By people I don't know to a woman I don't know and who is long dead. The cards she received once upon a time are now used as writing prompts.

"It's lovely," they say, "to know that my things are still being used. That they mean something, have a purpose." Do they really? Who will take over my furniture, my junk, my memories? My older son has dibs on the old restaurant chairs we used on two continents for hanging out and talking and on which my writing students now compose their stories. For his girlfriend I already packed the tea service from my grandmother.

Am I not too young to give up everything? On the other hand my experiences over the recent years showed me clearly that I cannot hold on to things. So, why not let go, deliberately and consciously? Saying goodbye has become easier. The idea of letting go of my possessions hardly scares me at all, compared to everything else I have lost. It even inspires me.

I am hardly alone. Since I've begun to think about it, I see it everywhere. The trend toward tiny houses. There are film clips on living in small houses, there are books, magazines, websites and blogs. The Internet community that collects tips and hacks keeps getting larger. Many were originally forced into reduced circumstances. Crises, loss of jobs, illness. Burn-out, the people's plague, turned more than one workaholic into a resident of a tiny house. Fascinated, I click through images for sheds, RVs, tree houses. I study the designs of Murphy beds, of bunk beds which fit whole offices underneath, of sliding doors and retractable kitchen counters.

That reminds me of an evening in Rotterdam where Lino, who studied architecture, did a semester abroad. He studied with a crazy genius professor who, among other projects, had a plan to move all of Holland's pig breeding farms into a system of tiers to save space. He asked his students to design an apartment that adapted to the resident's needs – by the hour. My son considered how an apartment with flexible rooms would look. When you got up at six in the morning the bedroom walls would retreat to the edge of the bed and thus enlarge the kitchen. Or the office. I remember sitting at the table in the flat he shared with other students and studying the plans. How I complained that there were no plans for a linen closet, no washing machine. Back then I wasn't a workaholic yet but I was overwhelmed by the demands of a household. I remember exactly how I felt when I studied the overlapping living spaces. Lino showed me a diagram that outlined what goes on in an apartment. The biggest area is dedicated to leisure activities. In the rooms designed by students there is laughing, dancing and music making, music listening, reading and relaxing. In the kitchen there is cooking and eating.

"And washing the dishes?" I ask. And immediately am ashamed of the question. It makes me old.

He shrugs, points to an area marked with very small print "maintenance" which covers all variations of housekeeping in one word. Even I, by no means hausfrau of the year, can think of many more terms for that than for the topic of leisure activities. The realization depresses me. Am I getting old? Yet the crazy professor who had the idea of flexible rooms is older than I am. It has nothing to do with age. Youth reveals itself in its flexibility not merely of the body but of the mind. The days I feel older than I am are those when I think nothing new is possible. Youth can only think in circles. "The head is round so thinking can change direction." This sentence also comes from an old man, Francis Picabia.

Do women age faster than men? At least mentally? If so, it must be because of those tons of obligations and expectations we carry around. Imagined or real. My obsession to keep the dream house intact didn't make anyone happy, least of all me. Today other items are listed among my duties which are probably equally pointless.

I asked myself back then, and I ask today: what do I need? A space to hang out. To be myself. A room of my own.

Thus I begin to say goodbye and at the same time enjoy my things, my plants, my pictures and books, my considerable collection of cowboy boots. Maybe more than before.

I could at least take the garden furniture, I think, while sitting on the terrace. Those rich colors would look good in the light of Santa Fe. Then I remember how much a container costs and discard the idea. The garden furniture will also look good elsewhere.

By the way, you can also live in a container. Not only involuntarily. I've seen it in a *Tiny-Homes* forum.

The Offer

The same evening I came back from the meeting with the financial consultant with a solution for everything George, not Natschler, but Nuescheler, the real estate agent from Santa Fe, wrote. He had a "highly motivated" buyer for my house who was willing to pay four hundred fifty thousand dollars cash. "I seem to remember," he cautiously writes "that after the debacle of the water pipes you were pretty sick of Santa Fe and the house." Where does that come from? I wonder and continue reading. "If I got the numbers right you'd end up breaking even, after taking off taxes and the notary, or maybe even a few thousand ahead."

I shut the laptop and look accusingly at the ceiling. What's all this about? Why today? Everything was clear. Decided. Solved. Now I suddenly have a second solution. I could act as if nothing had happened. "What? A house in Santa Fe?" I could say. "What are you talking about? Oh, THAT house in Santa Fe..." I would no longer be the bad daughter abandoning her mother, or a lousy mother abandoning her children.

"A divorced father who picks a new family, that's normal," a friend recently said to me. "But a mother who moves to the other side of the world – is not. That's not normal."

I could use the money from San Francisco for the rent in Aarau. It wouldn't cover my living expenses, but at least I could work less, go for walks, spend more time at the Zen-Center. I could stay in this lovely apartment, see the flowers on the deck bloom again next year, and the year after.

Is it a sign? Do I get the undeserved chance to right my wrong? Or is it a test? What is the best decision? I have no idea. What does my inner voice say? I can't hear it.

Instead, I hear the voice of Randa from nearly twenty years back, "what do YOU want?"

Not my mother. Not my friends. Not my publisher, my readers, my tax adviser. Not my sons –who, in fact, are for it. "You've got to do what's right for you," they say, very maturely. Even Mr. Perez from the bank is on my side, "it's your turn now," he says. "It's time to think of you." Suddenly I'm back at the beginning of this trip, the beginning of my idea. What is the best for me? What do I want?

My thoughts are going in circles. I don't hear an inner debate. I only hear demands rattling down on me from the outside. A twenty-one year-old isn't supposed to have to live without his mother. An eighty-year old woman should have her daughter nearby. Who knows how long your mother will remain alive? Only after she's dead are you allowed to think about yourself! And so on, and so on.

So I leave my thoughts and close my eyes. I imagine accepting George's offer. I see the sign again on Canyon Road, *Open House*, with an arrow pointing to the back yard. I imagine calling my mother and telling her. And her saying, "All is forgiven, beloved daughter! I will never be angry with you again."

Yeah, right! The image is absurd. But strong enough that my heart grows heavy and my eyes start to burn. Not from relief. Not from happiness. The familiar, heavy weight of oppression settles on me. It weighs so much I can hardly breathe.

"I'm sorry," I write back to George. "You misunderstood. My love for this tiny house is unbroken. It is not for sale." I press send and immediately feel better.

Ah, I think. I do know what I want. I just can't put it into words immediately. But I can thoroughly feel it. Clearly and unmistakably. George responds immediately. "As I said, my client is VERY motivated. In other words: Name your price!"

At which point the writer in me breaks through. "Sorry," I write, "My freedom has no price!" As grandiose as it sounds, it's true. The little house represents my freedom. To live my life. To make my own decisions. To write when and how much I want. The freedom to breathe thin air and look at stars.

Of course, this kind of freedom comes with a price. The goodwill and support of others. Not everybody, but many people close to me will not understand. I will have to learn to live without them. But I can breathe.

Only later I think of Frederic who so badly needed money and who did everything to convince me to buy. If he hadn't done that, if he'd hung on for another six months, he could have dictated the price to George's most motivated buyer. But it is what it is and it is good as it is.

A Pioneer in Winter

At the beginning of December I fly back to San Francisco. I have to go to court. The hearing is set for the second, the third I plan to continue on to Santa Fe. No matter what happens, my flight is booked.

In the weeks before my departure my fear grows. It feeds on the uncertainty because nothing about the situation makes any sense. I don't understand, I can't analyze it, my friends can't help. What appears plausible or right to us has no meaning in the eyes of the law. Common sense doesn't apply here – it is situations like these that make you aware of how lost you are in a foreign country. Even if you emigrate by choice, even if you're privileged. It's not easy to tolerate. I felt that often in our years in California. Emigration is not for the timid. Do I really want to face all that? Again? And this time all by myself?

Almost daily I call my lawyer and the insurance lawyer who tries to prepare me for the hearing. But I still don't understand why I should have to defend myself. I pack the most conservative outfit I can find in my closet. And several boxes of Sprüngli chocolates.

In San Francisco the sun shines, the temperature at five in the afternoon is still in the high seventies. Warmer than many of our Swiss summers. I peel off my fake fur coat and sweater. In the taxi I text my friend Theresa, "I'm on my way."

"Have a great flight!" she texts back. She thought I was landing the next day. She had just arrived at her friends' house across the bay where she had been invited to a crab dinner. Not wasting any time they pack the crabs, the sauces and the fresh sour dough bread into two coolers and the whole group returns to the city in the evening rush hour traffic. We all arrive almost simultaneously in front of Theresa's house. A short time later we sit around the table, sleeves rolled up, and with great concentration crack a mountain of crabs. A wonderful evening, uncomplicated, welcoming and full of ease. That has to be a good omen.

But when I appear at the lawyer's the next day, everything has changed.

"We'll settle out of court," he says.

"What does that mean?"

"We don't want you to stand trial. The risk is too great."

"I don't understand. I thought it was very important to show my face?"

"Yes, but..." I can see how difficult it is for him to formulate what he needs to say but just to be on the safe side, I pull one of the boxes of truffles from my bag.

"We can't tell how a jury will react to you."

"Me...?" I don't know what to say. What is there to say? "I thought I was the good guy... girl."

"Well, yes, but you know, the mood in the city is bad and has heated up in the last months. Everyone is suffering from those constantly rising rents..."

"I know." I too felt it this summer. And discussed it with my friends. But what does it have to do with me?"

"The people who can't excuse themselves from jury duty are precisely those suffering from these developments. We don't believe that you, as a homeowner, as a landlady who doesn't even live in the city, a foreigner from a rich country, can get the sympathies on your side in this climate."

I don't know what to say to that. I thought I was the victim. I never imagined I could be lumped together with riders of Google buses with tinted windows! Deep in thought I tear the wrapping off the praline box and put the first one in my mouth.

"And, what does that mean in terms of numbers?"

Joe gets thirty thousand dollars from my insurance. Which means from me. That bothers me. I consider it unfair, I rebel against it, and then I think: there is no appeal with a settlement. That also means it's finished. Over once and for all. That's the only thing that counts. The house is mine again.

I call a few friends, "we have to celebrate!"

But by the time I arrive in Santa Fe the next evening I'm exhausted again. This continuous fatigue is beginning to get on my nerves. This has to change! I made a detailed plan for my recovery: yoga and meditation, walks in the mountains. Eating healthy and dancing, getting drunk, laughing and falling in love. All that is on my list. And, of course, Christmas.

It is cold when I arrive at the airport in Albuquerque, and crystal clear. In winter the days are short, the stars glitter, the temperature stays around six degrees. I put my fake fur coat back on. For a fleeting moment I think, I don't like extreme temperatures! Then I'm in front of the car rental desk.

"Wouldn't you rather get an upgrade?" the clerk asks – but they always do that. And then it costs more. I don't fall for that any longer! "There will be snow," she says and I respond, arrogantly and stupidly, "Ah, you know, I'm from Switzerland. I know how to drive in snow." And besides I've been wanting to try out a Fiat 500 for a long time. The roads are dry and well lit. I make it to Santa Fe easily and I feel pretty good.

The house is welcoming. Doris came to clean the day before and just two days earlier the floors were put back. Over the new pipes and dry soil. I go for a short walk in the neighborhood, look in on Nathalie, the former fashion editor from Paris, and sit in the brightly embroidered armchair I love so much and that is so far out of my price range. And besides doesn't fit into the casita. A tiny house protects you from many foolish purchases.

I say goodbye to Nathalie without buying anything and continue on down to the Plaza. The trees are hung with lights, the air is sharp and cold. I didn't buy any groceries but I'm not in the mood to get into the car again and drive to the supermarket. At the bar of the Hotel La Fonda there is not much happening at this time of night. The musicians tune their guitars, a few tourists recover from shopping, the locals sit at the bar. A white haired woman with a flowery floor length dress from the seventies is drinking red wine and flirting with the bar staff. I sit near her. This could be me. In twenty years. After twenty years here. The image reassures me. I am in the right place.

During dinner I look through the local newspaper and what do I see? An intensive workshop with the pioneers of autobiographical writing, Natalie Goldberg and Julia Cameron. Authors I have wanted to meet for a very long time. Here in Santa Fe! The day after tomorrow! That very evening I make reservations. That is a good beginning.

I sleep badly; I'm not used to the altitude. Every time I wake up it seems colder in the house. The next morning I wake up and am completely snowed in. Along with my Fiat 500. And the heater's dead. At six degrees. I call Doris, Doris calls Jean-Francois, Jean-Francois sends two workers. They practically cross themselves when they see me. "Madre de Dios, is this house cursed?" They are the same men I've seen in the photos, the ones who dried Lake Milena and who dug out tree roots the size of elephant legs. They spent weeks here. And thought, as I did, that finally everything was all alright. But the heater is a different problem, though underground as well. There are only two vents in the floor where the heat comes out. And at this temperature that's simply not enough. But these temperatures are normal for Santa Fe. Thus, this problem, too, was known.

Last week before the freeze and while the floor was still up, it would've been easy to fix this problem. But now...

My old nemesis, Despair, comes to visit. She puts an arm around my shoulders, so heavy that my knees buckle and I drop my head. "You see, I told you, this is no good," she whispers. "You'll never be happy. It'll never be easy. Why don't you give up?"

She's never been so outspoken. I think her stupid stepsister, Exhaustion, is egging her on. But on my other side stands Doris who says, "that's normal. Something always goes wrong here. When I first moved here I had trouble for the first two years."

"Two years? And that's supposed to cheer me up?"

"No. For that we need strong coffee."

She drives me to the Coop on West Alameda, an alternative supermarket that sells only local produce and that sits right next to Doris's favorite cafe. The streets are not swept, the snow is supposed to melt during the course of the day. Until new snow falls. In the shady places the streets are iced up.

"Here you really do need a good car," Doris says. "A four-wheel-drive or something. Or else you're up a creek." But first we need coffee. As always, Doris is being hailed from everywhere. The snow is a common subject. "I didn't even drive to work today," we hear more than once. "You know someone who removes snow? Last week the guy charged me one hundred and sixty dollars, such a rip-off." Doris calls a client who lives in a remote area. "I don't know if I'll make it out to your house today. But, what was the name of the guy who shoveled your snow last week? He was good, right?"

That's how it's done. One person helps the next and Doris helps everyone. We buy groceries, candles, firewood and a blanket. When we get home the workers are gone. It feels as though the heat works again but when I check the thermometer, it shows 6 degrees. At least, above zero. I dress warmly and make a fire in the fireplace. I sleep on the sofa in the living room as it's closer to the warmth.

I decide to stay in the hotel the night before the workshop. My room is almost bigger than my house, and heated. And comfortable. I have a fireplace as well. A view to the snow covered hills. Over dinner I meet several great woman, among them Theo Pauline Nestor who organized the event. Twenty years earlier she worked as a waitress at the Teahouse on my street. Right where Nathalie Goldberg's *Writing in Cafes* takes place. I must be doing something wrong, she thought back then. I wanted to write. Not be a waitress! Today she teaches alongside her former idol. And in between she wrote a book about her divorce: *How to Sleep Alone in a King-Size Bed*. I have long mastered this one, but I particularly look forward to her workshop. It deals with the infamous *outline*, something I have always avoided in order not to curtail my pleasure at inventing. Let's see what I can do with it. I am open to anything and I like Theo who, when she was young, befriended two Swiss anarchists whom she went to visit. "Somewhere in the Canton Aargau, do you know the place?"

"That's where I live!" Ahh, small world! We drink another glass of wine and then order the snowmobile at the reception to bring us back to our rooms across the snowy paths. We wouldn't have made it by foot – because of the weather conditions, of course! I am very happy when I get into bed and look forward to the next day, the workshops, new faces, insights...

But when I wake up I'm no longer myself. A monster migraine has gripped me, something that had happened only three or four times in my life. I can barely get out of bed and get dressed, and in no way am I able to take part in a workshop. Guardian Angel Doris has to come pick me up and drive slowly, slowly back into town. At home I crawl into bed on all fours, where I remain for the next forty-eight hours in the dark, wanting to die.

But I don't die. The hours pass, I don't know if it's day or night, the room is dark. I lie in fetal position. I can't read, I can't think, and even breathing hurts.

Sometimes I hear voices. Every so often a shadow passes through the gloom. Katchie, Joshua and Doris take turns looking in, feeding the fire in the fireplace, bringing warm soup I don't eat. Katchie brings me two of her leftover, highly addictive, prescription pain pills that, unfortunately, don't touch the migraine in the least.

I whimper. When will it end? When will it get better? Discouragement sits on my chest as if I'd never battled it. Give up, give up, give up. One of four weeks is already gone and what have you achieved? Nothing. What of your lovely plans? Nothing.

"You're farther from happiness than ever," Despair comments impassively. I fidget, I cry, I fight. Try without success to squirm out from under her weight. "I am not a fox," I whimper. "I don't want to be a fox!"

My Zen teacher told me the story of the fox who didn't want to be a fox. "I have been reborn for five hundred lives as a fox," the fox complains. "When can I be a human again? How much longer?" Because the fox remembered the other life, the life as a human.

"Before you can be human you have to become a fox for real," was the answer. When I heard the story for the first time I got very irritated. Yeah, yeah, fine, I thought. I know what you want to tell me, what I'm supposed to learn, thank you very much! *But I simply don't want to be a fox*! Ever since the end of my marriage I only wanted one thing, to be over it. As fast as possible. Every tear I shed I experience as failure. I want to be happy, damn it, I want to be healthy, I want to be like new. I'm not getting younger, after all. I don't have time for suffering. Didn't I suffer enough before the separation? Before I could finally let go? Isn't that enough? And what's the deal with these physical ailments? At fifty I should be more fit than ever and more beautiful! That's what everyone says and everyone expects.

Instead, I feel every year doubly. I feel 102 years old. I fight my sadness, I hate my exhaustion. I battle with everything I have – which is not very much. And it is getting less all the time.

"I've been feeling like this for five hundred lives," I complain in the dark. I pray like a child, " please make it stop, please, please, make it stop."

At some point during the forty-eight hours I doze in the dark. I accept the possibility that nothing will change. That I will always be sad, always tired. If only the pain would ease up. And the nausea. And of course at some point that happens. At some point the snow melts. At some point I figure out how to stay warm with fire wood. And I have learned my lesson. I don't push myself any more. I jettison all plans, I cancel yoga, I stay at home. I move from the bed to the sofa and from the sofa to the window seat. It takes me forever to start the fire in the fireplace and I feel the deepest satisfaction when the smoke rises straight up and the flames envelop the wood. Some days I venture out for an hour into the bitterly cold beautiful fairy tale landscape. I walk the hundred yards to the Teahouse, I eat a sandwich, drink some coffee. I wander to the Plaza, visit one of the four museums that stands right next to each other. Just one. For an hour. That's enough. I go home and lie down. Maybe that's how it will be. Maybe I've turned into an old woman who can't do much. It doesn't matter. As long as my headache's gone! I don't really have to do anything – that becomes more and more clear. For short moments I forget that I've already found the solution for everything - surrender - and fall back into my old habit of punishing myself.

"I simply don't do anything," I tell Katchie. And she says, "Well, yeah, except for writing a book, a weekly column, turning in radio stories, a blog, responding to fan letters, doing your taxes..."

"OK, OK!" I can laugh at myself again. Twenty years ago I was celebrated as the "mother of the slattern movement. Over and over I encouraged women to ease up on themselves. Myself excluded, of course. Whatever I did, it was never enough. Never good enough. Even for my recovery I have a strict regimen, clear goals and am irritated at myself if I don't achieve them.

"You would never treat anyone as badly as you treat yourself" – I have heard this so often I don't even remember who said it first.

"Yeah, fine," I say. "I know. I am a fox."

We Are All Yetis: A Dream

I am alone. Alone in the world and the world is cold and white with snow. The ground is hard, I am wearing fur shoes, a fur coat, I am covered with snow – Nevada, the name of the main character in my novel, means "the snow covered one." At first I stand still, I breathe in the cold air that makes my lungs burn. I look around. My eyes tear from the cold air as much as from the certainty: there's no one, nothing. Suddenly a spoor opens in front of my feet, a solitary fissure in the endless white. I follow it and now the snow crunches under my furry feet; the farther I go, the clearer the trail and more and more footprints overlap. I walk the path so many have walked before, but I'm alone, all alone.

The earth curves. I can see it all the way to the end. I know that after the end something else comes, something new. I look to the right and sense the ocean. I could go to the shore, I think, I could go right and get to the sea. I imagine the wide blue expanse, the endless beach – I'd be just as alone but it would be warm. But for some reason I continue on to the left and there, behind a bend, behind the curve of the earth a completely different landscape suddenly opens up. I see it as if behind glass, like a mirage. A green summer meadow, knee high grass, wildflowers in all colors, an old tree with wide branches. A table stands underneath the tree, casually set, the plates don't match, the glasses are bulky. Huge platters of steaming pasta and salads, carafes of red wine without labels. It's one of those midday meals that go long into the afternoon. Children run barefoot around the table, the guests have moved the chairs, lean back, some have risen and exchanged places with others. They talk, laugh, kiss. Some dance farther down on the meadow. With yearning I look at this scene, how I would love to break through the glass, sit down at the table, belong. But I'm a Yeti from the ice, a fur covered being and the guests at the table are beautiful undamaged beings, slim and tan and all dressed in white.

And then it's as if my gaze of longing melted the glass, dissolved the barrier. I slink closer, taking a wide detour and checking the company constantly. Half of me fears they'll discover me, the other half hopes so. But I am invisible – as large, hairy and snow-covered as I am they don't see me. I become very sad. I knew there would be no space for me at that beautiful table. I'm ready to turn around, to retreat. Walking, I cast a last yearning glance at the table. The people are talking, laughing, eating without seeing me. I don't exist. I turn away – and see, all of a sudden, an old-fashioned wooden coat stand – and what do I see hanging on it? Tons of Yeti pelts! Snow covered furs, hats, overshoes! Exactly like mine.

I look over my shoulder at the table and only then do I see it: every single one of them still carries a bit of fur, on the hand, the foot, in the shape of a glove, a legging.

We are all Yetis I realize, a bit surprised, but relieved. I take off my pelt, hang it on the coat stand. Underneath I'm wearing a thin white nightgown. My legs are white. I keep on my gloves, I don't want to hide. I don't want to disown myself. I inhale deeply, stretch out my chin, step up to the table with my head high. It appears as if no one noticed me, still. But a chair has become available between two women, across from it sits a man. I sit down. They all speak with each other, turned away from me. I can't hear what they are saying, what they're speaking about, I can't insert myself into the conversation. Even the man across from me is not looking at me. But there is a waiter with a tray of glasses. I gesture and he sets a glass of red wine in front of me. I put my left hand, my bear claw, on the table. I wake up.

Feast of Love

Christmas is around the corner. The town fills. The population doesn't only grow in summer from eighty thousand to three hundred and sixty thousand. Over the Christmas holidays Santa Fe is overrun by tourists, and all those who have a 'second home.' Because Christmas is special here.

Not just here. Also in my life. Or, at least, since I had children. The first Christmas tree I ever bought myself was so small I could carry it home in the tram and it was decorated in pink from top to bottom. Balls, candles, glitter in neon pink. Lacking pink angel hair we draped a feather boa across the top branches. We shoved frozen cheese pies from the supermarket into the oven, turned up the music and opened the doors. With "we" I mean my roommate at that time and I. After I left home at seventeen, my friends and I had happily ignored Christmas and invented our own rituals, like binge-watching a surrealist Austrian mystery show all night long in a movie theater furnished exclusively with comfy old couches. But now I was twenty-four years old with a child, and Christmas took on new meaning. I couldn't offer my oldest son much: no real family, no stability, no mother who knew what she was doing. But there was one thing I could promise him: no matter where we are, no matter what happens, he will have Christmas at home – with both parents. And so it was. We celebrated in larger or smaller groups as our family expanded and shrunk again. We celebrated in America, in Switzerland, with small and large trees, with less and less pink decorations and more and more homemade ones, with English or German songs. We celebrated with everyone else who didn't know where to go, those who couldn't be home on Christmas Eve. When I was a young mother, none of my friends had children. Not for another ten years at least. They were still in adolescent mode. Some of them had strained relationships with their parents. So they came to our apartment and celebrated under the pink decorations. Later, after I remarried and had another son, we often had friends from abroad staying with us or foreign artists on a residency who didn't know anyone else in Switzerland. When we lived in San Francisco we would celebrate Christmas Eve with other Europeans. In short, we always celebrated together. A simple but nevertheless important ritual. For twenty-five years it made sense. Then it was over. The ritual had become empty. We repeated it one more time, because we didn't want it to be true. We thought it would be enough if we pretended. It wasn't.

I do it for my sons, I thought, grinding my teeth.

"We did it for you," they said later. "Because you love Christmas so much."

I didn't know what to say to that for quite a while. But I knew this couldn't be it. Rituals are important and beautiful. But they have to be filled with life to have meaning.

And then, last summer as I entered the casita for the first time, this absurd thought popped into my head. Here we could have Christmas together! At that time I didn't even know how Christmas is celebrated in Santa Fe. Together! All together, the whole town and the tourists who come especially for that. Santa Fe celebrates in the street – on my street! The whole Canyon Road is decorated with Farolitos, simple brown paper bags with some sand in the bottom and tea candles. Tens of thousands glitter in the clear air. By four in the afternoon people assemble on Canyon Road. Every restaurant, every cafe, every gallery, every residence opens its doors wide and offers food and drink. Everyone talks to everyone, everyone celebrates. Some people sing together. No one is alone.

This is how I want to celebrate Christmas. Together. With everyone. "You don't have to come," I tell my sons, "but this is what I'm going to do." This is my new ritual. It doesn't have to be theirs. But to my great surprise and pleasure they both sign up.

I feel stronger today. As if I passed a very long test. Like a pioneer who survived her first hard winter in a wagon. Not just the experience of being able to deal with all kinds of catastrophes, or the realization that a broken heart can be fixed just like a leaking water pipe. No, it is the recollection of the shadowy figures that scurried through my house. Those almost friends who looked after me, quietly and surreptitiously. I already knew I can take a lot. What I didn't know is that I can accept help.

"That's how it is here," Doris said. "Those who stay here, help each other." And the others move on. Behind the charming playful facade Santa Fe is a hard place. The thin air clears your head but it makes breathing difficult. The lovely light and wide sky challenge the lungs. The climate is extreme, either too hot or too cold and… "the worst you haven't even seen yet: spring! Oh, God! The dry desert wind blows constantly and everyone has hay fever."

The living conditions are just as extreme. The gap between the rich and poor is larger than in San Francisco where I had already found it hard to bear. There are those who literally fight daily for survival and those who chase after happiness. It's a place that attracts with its beauty, its deceptive light and that which only shows its face after a while. If you're only here for 'opera season' you'll never see it. I remember what Lil once wrote in her column "Coyote Corner" about life in the desert, "Whether in Africa, the near East or America, whether today or a hundred years ago – the deserts of the world seem to evoke similar thoughts and feelings in people. They all speak of the happiness the silence invites, the stopping of time, of the clarity of the gaze and a wholly different experience of nature and danger. And, of course, of being thrown back onto oneself – all things I've written about here as well. The desert has a way of very quickly spitting out those who don't belong. Someone told me that recently, a real estate agent funnily enough."

That's it. The desert chewed me up. But it didn't spit me out. With everything I discover daily, my certainty grows. I belong here. I'm happy here.

I can't explain it. Less and less.

I begin to prepare for my sons' visit. I'm nervous. I would be so pleased if they liked it here and, at the same time, I'm clear that it's not about that. I again have a whole list of things we can do together. Go skiing, practically next door. Supposedly it's not crowded, easy to rent gear and in half an hour you can be on the slopes. What a treat compared to the fancy ski resorts in Switzerland where the lines are endless and the prices steeper than the slopes! We could also go to the hot springs at Ojo Caliente and soak in the mud baths. Visit one of the nearby Pueblos, watch a ritual dance. Go to the movie theater that George R.R. Martin of *Games of Thrones* fame bought, renovated and runs at his own cost. As a gift to the community. And, of course, the Farolitos walk on the twenty-fourth of December. I gave up the idea of a Christmas tree in the Casita, there's simply no room. Instead I buy hearts cut out of sheet metal and attach them to the window. They twinkle with every breeze and when the light comes in, shadow hearts dance on the walls.

I put new sheets on the bed. Cyril is coming with his girlfriend. I'll leave the bed for the young couple. Lino and I will sleep on the two sofas in the living room. The house has no internal doors, if you need to use the toilet you have to pass right by the bed. Now I get worried. Will this work? Won't we get on each other's nerves? Should I have accepted Katchie's offer of letting Cyril and Mirjam stay in her guest house? But then they'd be so far away. I am selfish, I want them right here with me. If it turns out to be intolerable we can still figure something out. I unfold the table Frederic left behind. It can be folded into the wall. I set the table for their arrival. When it's time to pick them up, I have to crawl under the table to get to the door.

The streets are dry. I leave early because I want to exchange the Fiat 500 for a bigger and more snow-worthy car at the airport. As usual it takes me a while to find all the switches in the new car since I only learned to drive fifteen years ago, in San Francisco. I was so afraid then – these days I drive without a flinch halfway across the continent, by myself. At the exit I ask the guard whether my lights are on – the sun is still out in full force and I can't tell. But I know that in half an hour it'll be pitch dark.

"All good, ma'am," the old man says and holds up a thumb. I leave the rental car park, drive around three corners and back into airport parking. I'm way too early. The Albuquerque airport has become familiar to me, I know where to get the best coffee. I buy a newspaper I don't read because I'm staring at the stairs as if hypnotized. Finally they get here. I jump in the air like an American mother, I clap my hands, I yell loudly: "You're here!"

They let it pass. They look tired, the flight was long. We go into the parking garage and I can't find the car – I didn't pay attention to its make and model. I only remember what color it is. But the keys find it, making the lights flash in the dark spaces. We load two large suitcases and a backpack that weighs a ton into the trunk. None of this would have fitted into the Fiat. I pass out water bottles and give a speech about the altitude and lack of humidity. Cyril and Mirjam fall asleep immediately in the backseat. Lino sits next to me and is looking out the window. He's traveled widely and can get along anywhere. But out there there's nothing to see. Just dark night and traffic. I try to describe the landscape we're driving through and what it means to me.

"Mama, are you sure you've got your lights on?" he interrupts me, concerned.

"Of course I've got my lights on!" After all I did ask the parking attendant.

"But, mama, this guy's signaling you..."

I look over at the fast lane where a car keeps pace with me, the driver opens and closes his fist repeatedly, like flashing light, with a despairing expression.

"OK, OK!" I turn the switch one more rotation and the driver in the fast lane raises his thumb and disappears into the night. I hear my son breathe out, slowly.

"Oops," I say. And then I laugh though I notice Lino doesn't think it's funny at all. Already as a child he put himself in charge of our vacation budget and later, on the way to his American school, he was the one nervously keeping track of the gas gauge. Now he doesn't speak until we get to Santa Fe. I park in front of the house. It is so dark, so quiet, so cold. He gets out, stretches, looks around. Then he looks at me questioningly, like a botanist with a new species of bugs.

"Mama," he says, "you didn't even get upset!"

The new mother – a relaxed mother?

The house is instantly full. Bursting suitcases on the floor, cosmetic bags in the bathroom. There are not enough hooks for all the towels, not enough counter space for all the toothbrushes. The big coats, the boots and hats and gloves that are needed in this climate fill up the entrance. At the last minute I put up hooks in the door jamb. Our boots pile up on the floor.

We eat the Pizza Pouches I bought for Cyril, at the folding table that has to be put away after dinner because otherwise there's not enough space to sleep. Lino is newly in love, he calculates the time difference to Zurich, searches for a private space to talk on the phone. Good luck, I think. He goes outside in the bitter cold and soon returns with numb fingers. At some point we lie on our sofas, each with a laptop, with earphones on, and smile across the room at each other. Despite the earphones we hear the giggling from next door. I don't remember how long it's been since we've been this close. And I don't know why I was so worried. I don't remember the last time I was this happy.

The next morning I make bacon and eggs, an American breakfast. I move the comforters out of the living room, I make space for the table. It is like in a Zen center and it makes me laugh. Last year I spent a week in silent retreat and enjoyed it greatly. Only the meals were problematic for me. Eating together but each for himself. Everyone prepared their own meal, dealt with their own leftovers, washed their own dishes. This to me seemed nonsensical, cold and time-wasting. But that's how it was. And now I suddenly understand. It is good practice to do everything from beginning to end, not to leave things half way. To make the bed immediately after getting up, to wash the dishes right away, to put them immediately away, to store the table after eating.

The children who are no longer children suffer from jet lag. They listen to me with glassy eyes as I present my plans. They groan. "Skiing? Please, no. No sports."

"A mud bath? I didn't bring a swim suit..."

"Anything but sitting in a car!"

"I don't know about visiting a Pueblo, let alone observing a sacred ritual..."

"Is George R.R. Martin ever at the cinema? Will I get to meet him?"

Me and my lists, my intentions! I set them aside.

"What do you want to do?"

They look at each other, shrug. Preferably nothing at all. Just chill, hang out, rest up, be together. What more could a mother's heart want? The days pass slowly and peacefully. The small house miraculously offers enough space for everyone. The warmth spreads faster when the house is full. We discover environmentally-friendly briquettes made of coffee bean hulls that burn amazingly bright and long. We talk, we don't talk. Once in a while we go out to a cafe, to eat something, to look at store windows. I make them go to one museum, my favorite on the Plaza, the museum of Contemporary Native American Art. I've been there so often the volunteers at the counter and the gift shop know me. Patiently they answer my questions and they're happy to see me with others for once.

Lino begins doodling in his notebook, playing with ideas to add more storage space to my Casita. He ends up designing a wall unit for my bedroom, a combination bookshelf and closet that goes all the way up to the ceiling. Built around the bed. On the first draft he carefully includes the picture he gave me for my birthday, the world map, with the photos of him and his brother. He draws them as grinning stick figures. In all honesty, it is the most important piece of the drawing for me. Whether this shelf is a bit higher or that one wider is beside the point.

We are still family. We just don't look it.

And then it's December 24. My sons brought along the packages I've always put in their Christmas calendars. A tradition that I started when they were little, 24 little packages for each one. The tradition remains past their childhood, though the calendars now contain mostly useful things such as underwear and socks, but always and forever a little surprise mixed in. When Lino turned eighteen I asked tentatively if he wasn't a bit old for that? I'll never forget his look. I could just as easily have asked him if it were okay if I abandoned him at the freeway exit. So every November I start making up the calendars, forty-eight individual sachets that I structure like a short story. I interrupt the boredom of practical gifts with surprises. I build up to the grand finale in the last package. For twenty-five years it has always contained a Christmas trinket, an ornament that had something to do with our lives: a silver basketball, a glittering Golden Gate Bridge, a pair of skis, a musical instrument. Every year those new trinkets hang on our tree and tell our ongoing tale.

This year the packages inscribed with "24" contain Farolitos: paper bags, tea light candles, a bit of sand. We fix them up and set them on the window sill and the wall outside the house. On the street the preparations are underway. Volunteers fill thousands of paper bags with sand and candles. They'll be lit after sundown. Katchie comes by; she wants to do the Farolito walk with us. We open a bottle of Prosecco and out of the blue everyone brings out some small gifts. Cyril gives me a ceramic tile, where a female skeleton with stiletto heels and pink nails sits next to a pink phone on a table. Above it the words "Waiting for Mister Right."

"Cheeky devil!" Cyril grins. I bought everyone Zuni fetishes, carved stone animals that have influence on particular aspects of life. Bears for health, eagles for foresight, and, at this moment the most significant one: the snake that sheds its skin as symbol of change.

It's so cozy. We almost forget it's Christmas. Katchie jumps up, "the Farolito's walk has already started!"

We had almost forgotten it as well. We wrap up warmly and go outside. I hand out house keys in case we get separated. In my little house, in the backyard, we felt so secluded that the masses on the street take us by surprise. Right away we get separated. Indeed it feels like the whole town is here. Every store, every gallery is open. Something is being offered everywhere. On the sidewalk there are fires to warm the passersby. Here and there improvised choirs sing Christmas songs. People wear blinking reindeer antlers or Santa hats. Buggies are decorated with strings of Christmas lights, even dogs wear red velvet coats. Right off I lose sight of Katchie who later texts me that she escaped back home, it was too much for her. I drift, wave when I recognize someone, eat a cookie here, drink a cup of punch there. I, too, am soon overwhelmed by the crowds and retreat into my house. But I leave the door to the courtyard open so I can see the lights, hear the voices, the songs, the laughter and once in a while, a siren. I am alone but not alone. Everything is right here, directly outside my door. All I have to do is reach out. Right now I need nothing. It is all is right here – even here alone in my kitchen where I wash the glasses from the afternoon. I can always celebrate Christmas like this. It would even work when the kids are not here. It is obvious that they won't be able to come out here every year. They have fathers, grandparents, girlfriends, girlfriends who have families. They have their own ideas, their own plans. Christmas here has little or nothing to do with Christmas there, with earlier Christmases. It cannot be compared. That is exactly why it is possible. Bearable. More than that, it's beautiful. It fits. It suits this phase of my life. This might change again, of course. In fact, it very probably will. But I have stopped making plans.

One after another they return. They talk over each other, recount what they saw and experienced.

I find one more pizza in the freezer, shove it in the oven. No plates, just paper napkins. And here we sit, eat, laugh and talk all at once, until the jet lag catches up with them. Cyril crumples up the paper napkins and grins at me sleepily.

"Mama," he says, "this has been the most relaxing Christmas since… forever!"

www.ingramcontent.com/pod-product-compliance
Lightning Source LLC
Chambersburg PA
CBHW050411010525
26025CB00014B/826

* 9 7 8 1 6 3 4 9 1 9 0 2 9 *